# *A New Practical Guide to Rhetorical Gesture and Action*

53SP 26
May 2017

ISBN 978-0-9978664-0-7

Library of Congress Control No. 2017941782

Second printing, with minor corrections, March 2018

*A New Practical Guide to Rhetorical Gesture and Action* is published by 53rd State Press, 540 President St. #2E, Brooklyn, NY 11215. 53rdstatepress.org

# *A New Practical Guide*

TO

# *Rhetorical Gesture and Action;*

ADAPTED TO

## The American Drama:

from a work on the subject by H. Siddons,
itself adapted from M. Engel's German original

BY

## The National Theater of the United States of America

EMBELLISHED WITH THIRTY-SIX ILLUSTRATIONS
Expressive of the various passions as interpreted by some of the finest performers from the New York stage

*Illustrations by Jesse Hawley*
*with Commentary by Normandy Raven Sherwood*

*Prefaced with erudition by Dr. Dick Pricey*
*and a scholarly introduction by James P. Stanley*

First Edition, Unimproved

*53rd State Press*
*Brooklyn, 2017*

*If a pose or a gesture or a "move" recurs across time, what pulse of multiple time might a pose or a move or a gesture contain? Can a trace take the form of a living foot—or only the form of a footprint? Can a gesture, such as a pointing index finger, itself be a remain in the form of an indexical action that haunts (or remains) via live repetition? This is to ask: what is the time of a live act if the live act is reiterative? To what degree is a live act "then" as well as "now"? Might a live act even "document" a precedent live act, rendering it, in some way, ongoing, even preserved? An action repeated again and again, however fractured or partial or incomplete, has a kind of staying power—persists through time—and even, in a sense, serves as a fleshy kind of "document" of its own recurrence.*

—Rebecca Schneider

Performing Remains: Art and War in Times of Theatrical Reenactment

# Table Of Contents

# *Introduction: The New Age of the Actor*

By James P. Stanley

As a young avant-gardist entering New York's theater world in the late 1990s, I was often given to skepticism about actor training. Perhaps this was a defensive rejection of my recently completed training in classical theater at the London Academy of Music and Dramatic Art in a methodology that seemed so ill suited to the kind of work I now wanted to do. An angry kid from small-town New England, I had come of age in the angst-ridden, post punk music scene of the 1980s. And now, with my formal training in classical theater out of the way, I sought a return to the anti-establishment sensibilities and the DIY ethos that had first excited me about live performance. In becoming my own artist, I wanted to bring into the theater that combination of precision and abandon, of high values and low comedy, of speed, rage and idealism that were the hallmarks of bands like Minor Threat, Bad Brains, the Minutemen, whose records I owned, and other bands that I had experienced with visceral intimacy at the all-ages shows in nearby cities that I had gone to almost weekly in my teenage years. And so, despite all of my training at one of the world's elite theater conservatories, I came to the city with a robust suspicion of the morass of methodologies, teachers, coaches and training programs that assaulted young actors who aspired to commercial success, promising to increase their potential to "make it" in the biz. When actor training was not earnestly grounded in what I then saw as archaic theories of psychological realism and "the method," the rest of it seemed to comprise a parasite industry thriving on the swarms of actors that its host industry was unable to consume.

That I had founded my own actor training program, the James Stanley School of Very Much Acting, was a joke that I told with the National Theater of the United States of America (NTUSA), the company that I had founded with Ryan Bronz, Mark Doskow, Yehuda Duenyas, Jesse Hawley and Jonathan Jacobs around 2000. (We were joined a year or so later by Normandy Sherwood.) Our mission, consistent with the mock grandiosity of our name, was to poke serious fun at the self-seriousness of the art world, but also to treat the art itself seriously, as a mode of critique. At the time, we were all overcommitted, underemployed artists working in the tiny basement of a deli in Times Square through an informal residency we had with the arts group chashama. In naming the NTUSA we sought to evoke both the truth of our aspirations and the absurdity of our condition, and also to acknowledge our position—both geographically and ideologically—with respect to the show biz world that Times Square represented. Yes, we wanted to emerge from this dirty basement as a force on the global stage, to disrupt the Disnified engines of commercial spectacle overhead by offering something more daring and spectacular than they could possibly imagine—even as we slaved away without compensation, making our sets out of trash, and mocked by our own teenage interns. Embodying these contradictions, the National Theater of the United States of America represented, for us, so much of American theater itself: earnest, passionate, and as hubristic as it was ineffectual—the great Malvolio of the art world. And the company, as a whole, embraced that archetypal clown character even as we sought to blow it up, and to foment from its ashes a new mode of making meaning through performance.

The James Stanley School for Very Much Acting was an aspect of that character, the joke at the heart of which was that acting could easily be quantified in terms of less and more, and that somehow more acting was better acting. Demonstrations of Very Much Acting, as they played out in rehearsals and at post-show parties, depicted explosions of feeling, physicality and volume. And, as the joke evolved, our core curriculum in loud and fast acting styles was expanded to include our "Full Face Crying Workshop," and master classes such as Duenyas' "Art of the One Sided Telephone Conversation" and Jacobs' "Acting with Pointy Sticks." These jokes were both fueled by and featured in the shows we were making, which were themselves loud, fast and full of choices taken to absurd extremes.

In contrast to the stripped down aesthetics of Richard Maxwell or the cold technicality of the Wooster Group, the NTUSA took a maximalist approach. We found kinship in groups like Radiohole and the Collapsable Giraffe whose collaborative methods and raucous energy we aspired to. But we were less hardcore, less baldly confrontational. While they worked to evoke the punk nihilism of G.G. Allin and the perverse militarism of the Baader-Meinhof gang, we channeled our rage through Bob Fosse inspired dance numbers, vaudevillian stage antics, and Foreman-esque philosophizing in work that was tightly choreographed, frenetically paced and fun, playing out in disorienting, immersive spaces of light, set and sound.

But, however much fun we were having, I could not quite dismiss actor training altogether. The lampooning of my own training would not have been possible had I not found grounding in a new methodology more suited to the experimental work I was doing. New York experimental theater in the late nineties was awash in Viewpoints, a methodology developed by choreographer Mary Overlie in the seventies and adapted for the theater by Tina Landau and Anne Bogart in the following decade. Bogart had recently become head of the Graduate Directing Program at Columbia University and, through it, was producing a new generation of actors and directors whose sensibility seemed so different from the schools of naturalism and psychological realism that were the industry standards. And I was one in a pool of unpaid actors who worked with the program's directors on class assignments and thesis productions.

My initial exposure to Viewpoints, however, had come a few years earlier through my work with director Phil Soltanoff, whom I met when I joined the experimental Act One unit at the Williamstown Theatre Festival in 1996, and whose avant-garde sensibilities resonated with the discontent that I felt with the traditional theater and acting styles I had been trained in. Soltanoff had observed and worked with Bogart through her residencies with the SITI Company at Skidmore College, where he taught and directed as a visiting artist for more than a dozen years. Working with college students at Skidmore and aspiring professionals at Williamstown, Soltanoff had developed his own version of Viewpoints that suited his own aesthetic—a theatricality that dispensed with traditional narrative and character altogether in favor of more purely choreographic and musical structures. Not dance, but a theater of movement, form and image deeply informed by modernist experiments in indeterminacy by artists like John Cage and Sol Lewitt and postmodern minimalist composers like Steve Reich and Ryoji Ikeda. For me, Viewpoints, and particularly Soltanoff's bastardization of it, represented a wholesale release from the tyranny of the text, an escape from the flawed and tired logics of psychological realism and the "well made play" that had been the foundation of my schooling. While many of my peers had long been playing on this turf, for me it was an awakening to new potentialities where poetic logics, associative structures and kinetic assemblages could become the ground on which a whole theatrical universe could be built.

To be sure, Viewpoints did not escape our ridicule at the NTUSA. We often held "pretend Viewpoints" sessions as warm-ups and to break tension during our rehearsals. But in our play was an embrace of the giddy absurdity of the formal exercises, even as we mocked the self-seriousness that attached to the method as it made its way out of the academy and into New York's theater making scene. These "pretend" sessions were an extension of the culture of riffing and improvisation that we cultivated as the engine of our early work. The more completely we gave ourselves over to the rules of the exercises, the more we were able to find each other as performers within that structure and to play in it with abandon. And while none of us would have admitted Viewpoints as central to our method of making work, and despite our mocking resistance to it, we were no less informed by our exposure to it.

Several years later, after the Very Much Acting joke had run its course, Normandy Sherwood gave Jesse Hawley a stack of photocopies as a birthday gift. The photocopies were images from Henry Siddons' 1807 illustrated actor's guidebook *Practical Illustrations of Rhetorical Gesture and Action*. And this book immediately resonated with us on many levels. First, as an aesthetic object it seemed almost made for us, in the dramatically posed figures that it presented, but also in its too-long title and the lofty, pedantic tone that Siddons struck in his text. This was a tone we strove hard to achieve in our website, press copy and other forms of self-documentation, flush as we were in the mock seriousness of our mock national enterprise. But more importantly, as an historical artifact, the book seemed to describe an alternate theatrical universe guided by a set of formal rules that, to contemporary sensibilities, seemed patently absurd, even as they were presented as self-evident.

The NTUSA had, by this time, created several shows that mined historic forms of entertainment and spectacle, each time taking formal genres—vaudeville and early film comedy in *Garvey & Superpant$*, casino floor shows in *Placebo Sunrise*, self-help seminars in *Superconfidence*™—as a structure in which to improvise and play. And essential to our play was an acknowledgment of the rules of each genre and the ways in which the logics of these genres, seemingly natural in their historic moments, had become strange over time. Our characters were often trapped in these generic constructs and conscious of the ways their trajectories through these worlds were structured for them, even if they didn't totally understand the rules themselves. These were characters whose sense of free will was always at stake. And whether they resisted or engaged with the worlds they inhabited, the drama, comedy and tragedy for each of them lay in the inevitability of events that each saw coming but were unable to avoid. Despite their will to rebel, our characters could not resist the telling of a joke, the performance of a dance, the enacting of a murder, even as they foresaw the grim consequences it would often have for them. Read in this context, Siddons' book of gestures, and the mind-body disconnect his theory required of his actors, seemed to us a ready field to play in. But we didn't want to make a show from it. Instead we became interested in the book as a guide for young actors.

Siddons' instructional tome threw into historic relief the conviction of so many schools of thought that sought universal answers to the historically persistent problems of acting in the theater. As a manual for the working actor it seemed to offer the impossible: a concrete methodology to attain "perfection" in theatrical expression, honoring the traditional theatrical values of narrative and character, but from the outside in, rather than from the inside out. Siddons' theory seemed to represent the inverse of Stanislavski-based approaches that had been dominant throughout the twentieth century and in which we all, at least to some extent, had been schooled. Instead of action emerging from some achieved interior truth that the actor mined from her own experience in communion with the text, correct action, Siddons argued, could be achieved through access to a finite menu of universal human gestures applied appropriately to theatrical moments. Like our own school of Very Much Acting, it offered a preposterously mechanistic prescription for a process that conventional training had taught us was emotionally deep and psychologically complex. But despite its archaic mode of argumentation, Siddons' theory itself seemed to resonate with contemporary methods, like Viewpoints and our own creative processes, that turned away from human psychology and emotion and privileged instead formalist aesthetics, imagistic modes of presentation and the pure theatricality of bodies taking shape in space. And so we saw in Siddons' work aspects of our own.

Our thought then became to produce an updated book of rhetorical gestures in which we would ask contemporary performers to reinterpret gestures from the original. As in our shows, our goal would not be to simply lampoon the original. Nor had we a singular theory of acting that needed articulation and to which these images would function as an index. Rather, we hoped we could arrive at an index of gestures that represented the multiplicity of performers and performance styles that we saw at work in our community. And in doing so, we saw an opportunity to create an historical artifact of our own by documenting the community of theater makers of which we felt ourselves a part.

Theater is, after all, one of those ephemeral art forms that leaves only traces of its material presence behind. Theater's very ephemerality, according to theorists like Peggy Phelan and Herbert Blau, is part of its ontology. And, as Matthew Wittmann, curator of the Houghton Library Harvard Theatre Collection, explained to me, the archives for contemporary experimental theater are extremely thin, either because avant-gardists don't have the resources—the time, the space, the personnel—to build and keep their own archives, or because so much of contemporary work is developed through digital means, and archives like Harvard's haven't yet developed adequate systems for archiving digital media. Where traces of the avant-garde are available are in founding documents filed with state and federal agencies, reviews of the work in the popular press and in arts journals, critical assessments of the work in books and academic journals, grant applications to funding agencies and foundations, and in the artists' websites and promotional materials. And one could, if immersed in this data, sketch the outlines of an experimental theater community such as ours. But, in this project, we saw the opportunity to do so concretely, to create an artifact that would testify to our own community at this moment in performance history and that could be a piece of art in its own right.

*Practical Illustrations of Rhetorical Gesture and Action* was first published in 1807, in the midst of what theater historians often call the age of the actor. Written by Henry Siddons—actor, theater manager and son of the great Sarah Siddons—the book was a quite literal translation of a German treatise on acting, published in 1785, by J.J. Engel, director of the National Theater of Berlin. Its subtitle, "Adapted to the English Drama from a work on the subject by M. Engel, member of the Royal Academy of Berlin," shows both Siddons' attention to these debates and his ambition for his own work to be taken seriously not only by actors who might find it practical—that is, useful for their work on stage—but also through its vetting by Berlin's Royal Academy. While Siddons professed that he had adapted the original for the London stage, that "adaptation," according to historian Shearer West, consisted largely of changing the figures' heads to those of British actors, specifically those of John Kemble and Sarah Siddons, his uncle and mother, widely considered the greatest actors of their day. Young Henry may have been hitching his wagon to the family star—having withering success as an actor on the London stage in the early eighteen-aughts, by 1809 Henry had relocated to Edinburgh where he would devote himself to theater management. But with this book, published in the midst of his brief acting career, Siddons made a bid to be taken seriously in the theater world by entering an ongoing debate.

Since the 1740s, debates about proper approaches to acting had been playing out in a multitude of treatises that came cascading out of Italy, France, Germany and England, a flood of theorization that persisted well into the nineteenth century. Within this debate, Enlightenment principles of scientific rationality were countered by Romanticism's privileging of embodied emotionality and individualism. On the one side were theories describing acting as a science, whose rules could be mastered and which left no room for the spontaneity of felt emotions. On the other were theories that championed embodied emotionality as the key to lifelike verisimilitude on the stage. Sainte-Albine's Le Comédien (1747), Riccoboni's L'Art du théâtre (1750), John Hill's The Actor: A Treatise on the Art of Playing (1750, a translation of Le Comédien), G.E. Lessing's Hamburgische Dramaturgie (1767), and Denis Diderot's The Paradox of the Actor (written in 1773, but not published until 1830) all came down on one or the other side of this equation, favoring either intellection or emotionality as the proper guide to mastery of the craft. And while the above giants set the terms for the debate, that debate was carried forward by a still wider spectrum of writers—including playwrights, journalists, academics, aristocrats, lawyers and actors themselves—who wrote articles, essays, letters, treatises and volumes on actors and acting, championing one perspective or another.

As its descriptor would imply, the age of the actor was renowned not for its plays but for its performers. And the newfound popularity of theater and the profusion of theories on acting were only part of the equation. In England, one of the centers of the theatrical world, the cultural significance of the actor intensified with the passage of the Licensing Act of 1737, a draconian attempt by the English royal authority to stem the steady flow of popular plays lampooning the hypocrisies of the ruling class. In accordance with the Licensing Act, all theaters in London were closed with the exception of two—Drury Lane and Covent Garden—and all new play scripts required government review prior to production.

As a result, few new plays were produced, London's two sanctioned theaters preferring to rely on tried and true classics rather than risk costly governmental rebuke. And, in turn, both critical and popular attention fell from playwrights of original fare to actors' interpretations of plays from the Elizabethan, Jacobean and Restoration canons.

This turn in attention from playwrights to actors coincided with a boom in print and visual media that were increasingly available to the widening publics of Europe. Accordingly, critiques of actors' performances and details on their private lives began appearing in newspapers, novels, literary and political journals, and gossip rags. And their likenesses began appearing in a variety of visual media, including portraits, prints, etchings and engravings. These images of actors sometimes appeared in print media, but were more often sold and circulated on their own, either as individual art works (and copies thereof) or printed on such novelty items as mugs, pottery figures and porcelain tiles so that fans of these actors could purchase them as keepsakes.

The effect of this boom in print and visual media—its foregrounding of actors and actors' lives in the cultural scene—was that it fostered in this newly mediatized public a sense of public life as a kind of performance in and of itself, and of the world as a kind of stage on which dramas, public and private, were ceaselessly playing out. Richard Sennett's seminal book on urban modernity, *The Fall of Public Man* (1974), describes at length the centrality, in the public mind of eighteenth century Europe, of the figure of the actor as proxy for the new urban citizen. And a recent double issue of the scholarly journal *Eighteenth Century Fiction* details the ways in which "theatrical experience [was] embedded in the mediascape of London, the provinces and the colonies," elaborating on the ways in which theater had become a "crucial media hinge" through which all social and cultural phenomena were remediated and processed by their audiences.

The extent to which developments in media provide communities with new ways to think about performance—both theatrical performance and the performance of everyday life—is perhaps an argument for a different essay. But I introduce it here to suggest a parallel between Siddons' theatrical culture and our own. Both are scenes in which massive shifts in the number and type of media platforms citizens have access to coincide with changing notions of what it is to perform one's identity publicly and how that differs, or doesn't, from one's private persona. While Siddons' culture offered citizens a metaphorical platform whereby actors and other celebrities became media proxies through which people could vicariously live their lives, contemporary digital culture offers each of us a multitude of media platforms where our identities proliferate in as many variants as we choose to produce. Which is to say that in both of these media cultures performance becomes a site of contestation where ideas about interior truth and exterior appearance, embodied and projected identity, and attendant ideas about authenticity in representation are called into question.

The most famous actor of the late eighteenth century was David Garrick who, a few years after the passage of the Licensing Act, emerged as England's premier interpreter of Shakespeare, revolutionizing acting with his naturalistic approach. Supported by theorists like Saint-Albine and later John Hill, Garrick embraced the concept that true verisimilitude required that an actor *feel* the part. A good actor, writes John Hill in *The Actor: A Treatise on the Art of Playing* (1750), "must feel everything strongly, that he would have his audience feel: in order to his utmost success, it is necessary that he imagine himself to be, nay that he for the first time really is, the person he represents." While Garrick and his protégés enjoyed great success, critics of this new style wrestled with the degree to which conscious judgment could be brought to bear on a performance by an actor so lost in his part, and derided their naturalistic performances as lacking in art and in conscience.

For such critics, John Kemble and Sarah Siddons offered a solution. Their classicism was not so much a return to the cold declamatory style that Garrick had rebelled against, but rather an investment in a heightened form of realism which replicated not the quotidian gestures of everyday folk, but rather their ideal forms as embodied in classical painting and sculpture. We can again look to Shearer West who, in his 1991 book on the visual culture of eighteenth century theater, The Image of the Actor, writes of Sarah Siddons, "[her] perfection did not consist so much in knowing the character intimately as acquainting herself with the picturesque possibilities of the passions expressed by that character ... [and applying them] in such a way that they would be both accessible to her adoring public and deliberately evocative for art connoisseurs—inevitably a large proportion of her audience." And with *Practical Illustrations of Rhetorical Gesture and Action*, Henry Siddons emerged as a champion of this new classicism.

Siddons' book is written as a series of personal letters in which the author defends his proposal for a classicist treatise on acting against a (hypothetical) critic who warns that "every thing which is executed by *prescribed rules* will be *formal, stiff, embarrassed* and *precise*." By the third "letter," however, the critic is miraculously convinced. "How is this?" writes Siddons, "You! You who, a short time ago, laughed at my theory, as absurd and impracticable, now give me the greatest encouragement to proceed with my plan." Siddons then goes on with his plan, chapter by chapter, to address the various passions that a player might be called upon to play, and how she might achieve perfect expression of said passion through physical gesture, relayed in great detail and often with variations adaptable to a multitude of situations. For instance, of "Disdain" Siddons writes:

> *Marks of disdain are the turning away from a person, or looking at him aside, darting a quick glance with a haughty air. Sometimes with the head turned over the shoulder, as if the object were unworthy of a more serious or attentive examination. It often happens that the expression of disgust is superadded, by a turning up of the nose, and a slight elevation of the upper lip. And when the despised object seems to entertain too high an opinion of himself, and wishes to oppose pride against our judgment, the eye then measures him with the glance of raillery, while the head inclines a little on the side, as if, on account of our height, we found a difficulty in comprehending all the littleness of our opponent.*

While such a textually ungrounded, purely formalistic approach to acting may strike contemporary readers as silly or insipid on the one hand, or inspired experimentalism on the other, it turns out Siddons, as an actor and a budding theater manager, may have had practical ends in mind. Siddons' theory was one of the first to draw attention away from the face of the actor and to the whole of his body as a means of addressing the demands placed on the actors by the then recent expansions of the Covent Gardens and Drury Lane theaters. In other words, in these newly capacious theaters, where the story might be familiar but the text might not even be heard by those in the upper galleries, the images created by bodies on stage might have been more useful as a mode of storytelling than the actors nuanced interpretations of the text which might be lost in the distance. This is not to suggest that Kemble, Siddons, et al., were not great interpreters of text in their own right, but rather to suggest a pragmatism to the shift in critical attention away from the actor's interpretation of the text and toward the shape of the actor's body in the whole of the mise-en-scène.

To be sure, the conditions for experimental theater in twenty-first century New York are nothing like those of the Georgian stage. Here, playwrights are plentiful, and celebrated for their originality; governmental censure, despite continued attacks on the NEA, has little power to silence artists outright; stages abound, and those used for experimental performance tend toward the intimate for reasons both practical and artistic. And, as entertainment media has proliferated over the past two hundred years, theater has long ceased to be a central pop cultural concern, experimental theater even less so, as its actors are rarely covered in the popular press unless they have crossed over into other more prominent media. Finally, if, according to conventional narratives of western theater, the *age of the actor* gave way to the *age of the dramatist* around the turn of twentieth century, by the end of that century the dramatist/playwright would compete not with the actor, but with the director for billing as primary visionary in the theatrical arts. And yet, within the experimental theater community that I know, the actor has never been more important, not only in bringing to life the artistic vision of any particular dramatist or director, but as iconoclastic artists in their own right around whom productions are built, and in the expanded capacities in which they often contribute as multi-disciplinary artists to any given production.

The artists represented in these pages are the inheritors of a legacy of revolt that extends to the theatrical avant-gardes of the turn of the last century, but which took hold with renewed vigor in the late sixties and early seventies. Part of a wider cultural revolution that rejected bourgeois modes of art and art consumption, this movement called into question long held theatrical conventions, including that of theatrical naturalism. Indeed, if these two theater cultures can be likened in any way, it is in the alignment of the pendulum swing within these cultures from the dominance of one approach to acting to the *influence* of the other—by which I mean that in neither case was there a wholesale abandonment of the text or the principles of emotionally grounded acting, but rather that in both there was renewed investment in the externality of form as a complement to internal, felt emotions.

Of course, naturalism as a formal theatrical genre only took shape in the late nineteenth century with the plays of Strindberg and Ibsen. But its dominance as a standard for theatrical representation has lasted even into the twenty-first. Throughout this time it has been the purview of one avant-garde after another to challenge this aesthetic by offering alternative modes of theatrical expression. Historian and theorist Erika

Fischer-Lichte writes of theater as operating in both "referential" and "performative" modes. And while the "referential function deals with the representation of figures, actions, relationships and situations," as in conventional fourth wall drama, "the performative deals with the realization of actions" by both actors and audience in the shared space of the theater, what she describes as "the 'eventness' of theater." Throughout the long twentieth century, she argues, one avant-garde after another challenged the dominance of theater-as-representation by reframing theater as event, as festival, as ritual, as spectacle, as happening and as community action.

Despite the persistence of these techniques-cum-critiques, the dominance of theater as representation has remained strong. As late as 2004, Bogart and co-writer Tina Landau lament in their Viewpoints handbook the persistence of naturalism as a dominant theatrical aesthetic, attributing it largely to the pervasive influence of Stanislavski, or rather the "misunderstanding, misappropriation and miniaturization of the Stanislavski system" particular to the United States, in what would come to be known as "the method."

When Stanislavski and the Moscow Art Theatre arrived in America in 1924, we should remember, they were themselves considered an avant-garde, offering relief from the melodramatic and romantic styles of the nineteenth century that had come to seem archaic in the new theater and media cultures of the twentieth. European strains of naturalism had already begun to influence playwrights in America by the turn of the century, but it was not until Stanislavski's arrival in the West in 1924 that actor training began to catch up. Stanislavski's methods, emphasizing ensemble production and actors' long term work on themselves, would prove applicable to many different genres of performance. But, in its appropriation in America it was linked specifically to psychological realism, an emergent theatrical style that would become dominant in acting across media including film and television for the duration of the twentieth century. Stanislavski would go on to critique his own early work, later promoting theories of actor training less specifically attuned to realistic representation. But his method stuck, spread first through the writings and teachings of his students Richard Boleslavsky and Maria Ouspenskaya, and in turn by their students who would found the vastly influential, if short lived, Group Theater in 1931, and later the Actors Studio. So impactful was Stanislavski's legacy, so strong was realism's hold on American performance culture that by the mid-century, method based training was virtually the only type of training available.

But realism was not the only enemy of the late twentieth century avant-garde. Rather, realism was merely one among many bourgeois theatrical conventions that this culture of revolutionaries understood to represent the capitalist, conservative, patriarchal and authoritarian power structures that were the engines of their generation's unrest. Other targets included the primacy of the play as literary text, the authority of the director, the commodification of art in general and the institutionalization of artistic cultures. Against these forces they pitted new forms of theater that were by turns openly political, aesthetically subversive, democratically inclusive and celebratory of the "eventness" of theater that Fischer-Lichte described and that conventional bourgeois theater in the sixties seemed to deny.

Theater historian Marvin Carlson describes theatrical avant-gardes since the 1960s as developing in two distinct directions. In the first, exemplified by such directors as Robert Wilson and Richard Foreman, individual visionary auteurs, dispensing with traditional text-based approaches to theater making, became "creators of their own total theatre world." In the second, exemplified by companies like the Living Theatre and Schechner's Performance Group, the work was not the manifestation of any single visionary artist but rather emerged out of the collective vision of the group, including actors, writers, designers, dancers and other artistic collaborators. While these models may be useful in describing the polar extremes of artistic collaboration, such categorization belies the degree to which, in so much contemporary work, lines in the division of labor have become fluid. For instance, Young Jean Lee, widely considered one of America's leading auteurs, maintains tight authorial and directorial control of her plays. Yet her development process is at times deeply reliant on the actors with whom she works, often longtime collaborators, who generate material driven by her prompts, which she then sculpts into a performance text. On the other hand, groups like Radiohole and our own company, who have at times aspired to pure non-hierarchical collaboration, have often given over, and willingly so, to more traditional divisions of labor, sometimes acknowledged and sometimes assumed, often out of sheer convenience or necessity.

My point here is not to expose these artists or the models that they (or we) represent as false. Nor is it to make the rather uninspired point that all theater-making is inherently collaborative. It is, rather, to emphasize the expanded collaborative and creative roles that actors in the world of experimental theater so often play, and the virtuosity that they so often display in a multiplicity of creative capacities. A look at the biographies of the actors in this book reveals nearly all to be multidisciplinary artist who, while acting in a piece might also write, direct, choreograph, design and build sets, design costumes, video, lighting and sound, or develop new technologies and software for the stage. It is here that the stereotype of the actor, waiting tables and performing in showcases until he can break into the biz, fails to translate to the avant-garde world. In the avant-garde world, there is no biz to break into. There are circles of funders, presenters and artistic cliques that can offer expanded opportunities for participation and exposure. But there is no "other side" (short of a MacArthur Award) where working theater artists can stop worrying about their bottom line and focus only on their chosen discipline, even if they wanted to. And so, for some of us, multi-disciplinarity becomes a way to eke out a living while staying engaged in the theater and expand one's opportunities for creative collaboration through a network of labor relations.

But multi-disciplinarity is also a choice. The discontent I felt with the wider world of theater when I first moved to the city had as much to do with the content of the work being produced on conventional stages as it did with the actor's position in the production of that work. As a commercial actor I knew I would be last to be paid and first to be replaced, but still, I was told, lucky for any opportunity for exposure. In my poorly compensated day job as a "reader" for a top New York casting agent, I cringed not at the parade of actors that came through the door to audition for parts in Broadway plays and musicals, but at the conversations that were had when they left. It rankled me to be referred to as "an actor," not because I lacked respect for those who identified as such, but because I was dismayed by the conventions of an industry that treated a whole class of artists as expendable commodities rather than artistic collaborators.

Some artists are able to separate their work life from their acting life, and see in that separation a freedom from the influence of economic concerns on their artistic production. As a guest lecturer in our 2009 show Chautauqua!, Juliana Francis-Kelly (see fig. 9: Horror) describes her early trajectory in New York like this: "When I graduated from acting college it was my goal to never get paid for acting in the American theater. I decided that I would work a series of ridiculous side jobs that would allow me complete freedom to work for brilliant insane people for absolutely no money. None of these side jobs would require any skill or talent that might suck any energy away from the freedom of [making theater for] no money." Francis-Kelly would become downtown royalty through her work with Reza Abdoh, Richard Foreman and others, but would also expand her practice to include writing and directing her own plays.

My own trajectory was less focused. As noted above, I was late to the avant-garde game. Coming out of a traditional acting school and being confronted with the illness of my fit within the conventional theater world, I decided to become a maker of my own work, and I pursued it with adolescent impatience. I did work meaningless jobs, but I took my aspirational cues from the post punk music makers whose DIY ethics I aspired to, and which I saw at work in the theater companies that I admired. As Minutemen bassist Mike Watt notes in *Our Band Could Be Your Life*, Michael Azerrad's book on the indie music scene of the 1980s, that scene was about "more than just starting a band. It was starting a label, it was touring, it was taking control." In the downtown theater world, taking control meant learning all the parts. It meant starting a company and becoming your own writer, producer, designer, performer and technician. It meant lending these skills to other artists in whatever capacity you could to make their shows work. It was about participation in a community of exchange and support. So, while my peers may still have thought of me first an actor, I strove hard to cultivate a multi-disciplinary practice and considered that multi-disciplinarity an essential component of my artistic identity.

So it is no small bit of cheek for us to describe this book as an actor's guide. Like the original, it is a catalog of theatrical gestures that can be applied to various dramatic situations offering advice on how they can be used in the practice of acting. But it is also a catalog of actors who we understand to represent the forefront of the craft of performance. And it is a celebration of these performers as multi-disciplinary artists, as artists who embody the contemporary ethos of collective creation. And, in that, it is our salute to a new kind of *age of the actor*.

In terms of acting proper, Stanislavski's system has not lost its dominance nor its utility in the new millennium. But it is by now largely recognized as a child of the twentieth century. It is still taught almost universally, but often in tandem with other modes of training that attempt to balance his approach (or rather that of his disciples) with other modes of physical, vocal and sensory training. Meanwhile, those on the forefront of theatrical experimentation have begun to ask a perhaps misleading question: what's next?

*"For more than a century the dominant technique for acting has been based on Stanislavsky, The Method and psychological realism. How do actors do what they do in a post-Freudian, post-psychological, mediated world of ensemble and collaborative work, postdramatic theater, contemporary performance, and multimedia immersive experiences?"*

So began the description of a roundtable discussion held as part of the Public Theater's 2015 Under the Radar Festival entitled "The Art of Acting in Contemporary Theater." The roundtable featured an A-list of performers working in contemporary experimental theater, several of whom are featured in this volume. What the discussion revealed, however, was not an emerging methodology for the theater of the new millennium, nor even a summary rejection of Stanislavski's techniques. Indeed, many of the discussants received formal training in various strains of "the method," and valued their training, at that. Instead this discussion revealed a panoply of individualized methodologies cobbled together from both formal training (eclectic in its varied combinations of traditional and experimental techniques) and experience in the field.

That there should be a "next," that some single dominant methodology should come to take the place of Stanislavski's system, I would argue, is an ideological holdover from the reign of that system. Perhaps what is next is, and should be, a return to what we've had all along among actors whose careers have demanded wide ranging flexibility: a makeshift jumble of complementary and contradictory methodologies, some solidly grounded in theory and formalized through their implementation in institutional training programs, others arrived at through individual practice, observation and adaptation, as in the system of apprenticeship that predated actor training in the west. As represented by the actors in this book, it is along the fault lines between these many methodologies, ranging from immersion in some psychological reality to the aping of physical form to the pure pleasure of play on the stage, that productive tensions arise, and through whose frictions the theatrical space in contemporary theater is set alight.

## Our Method

This project is an attempt to document the community of theater artists that we have felt ourselves a part of over the past twenty years. But while we have aspired to represent this community on these pages, we cannot claim to have done so in a way that is either comprehensive or objective.

Like any documentary project, ours is limited by our own subjectivity, by the resources at our disposal and by the time we gave ourselves to complete it. A labor of love, this project focuses specifically on performers who have affected us personally, who we have worked with at one time or another or who we have seen work again and again, and who have unceasingly inspired us. On a more practical level, this project was limited by our access to those who were in town when we were in town, who responded to our emails, or who crossed our paths at fortuitous moments throughout the two and half years of its production. In short, as many performers as we have been able to represent here, we regret that we have left out so many more. And to all of you, we tip our hats with sorrow and with longing.

The actors who do appear here gave us their time and indulged us in our whimsy. They plumbed their imaginations for the poses they struck and offered us insight and inspiration in our conversations about the project. And they spread the word, inspiring faith in and garnering support for this project in the wider world. And to all of these artists we are deeply indebted. In addition to those who do appear here, there are a few souls who generously posed for us, but who, for one reason or another, we were not able to include in this volume. And so to Jason Craig, Jessica Jelliffe, Matt Korahais and Emily Davis, we owe you a debt of gratitude and several beers.

For each image in this book we assigned our performers a gesture from the original and asked them to interpret it as they saw fit. In each case, we showed them the original gesture, and in some cases offered them a number of images that we thought related. Some performers chose to reproduce the gestures in the original as exactly as possible. Others preferred to improvise. We also gave them the option of costuming themselves in accordance with the image, with their ideas on the gesture, or to simply work in their street clothes. Responses were as varied as the performers themselves. While most performers indulged in the exercise, others resisted, all of which we sought to capture in the illustrations here.

The actors were first photographed in a studio. Jesse Hawley took the photos, then transformed her photographs into illustrations, drawing on the tradition of theatrical portraiture popular in Siddons' day. Hawley's illustrations, ranging in size from 12 x 18 inches to 24 x 36 inches, were then digitized and printed in full scale on archival paper. Working by hand, Hawley applied color to some aspect of each of the prints—a process that was not part of the original, but which we observed in other illustrated books of actors that we found at the Harvard Library. As in Siddons' original, each illustration in the book is paired with text musing on the gesture and its utility in various stage situations. This commentary, written by Normandy Sherwood, is in many cases based on interviews with the actors conducted after their photos were taken. Sherwood gestures toward the original with her mock pedagogical tone, but adds to it a wry poetic lightness, opening a space for contemplation.

Like many of the NTUSA's works, this one starts with a joke. But also, like many of our works, we hope that it is beautiful to behold and useful to think with. As the company's final project, we offer it as a love letter to the community of artists who have sustained us, and who continue to inspire us to create new work.

For further reading please see:

Michael Azerrad, Our Band Could Be Your Life: Scenes from the American Indie Underground, 1981-1991. Boston: Little, Brown and Company, 2002.

Anne Bogart and Tina Landau. The Viewpoints Book: A Practical Guide to Viewpoints and Composition. New York: Theatre Communications Group, 2005.

Marvin, Carlson, "Postdramatic Theatre and Postdramatic Performance." Brazilian Journal on Presence Studies 5:3 (September/December 2015).

Eighteenth-Century Fiction 27:3–4 (Spring–Summer 2015).

Erika Fischer-Lichte, "The Avant-Garde and the Semiotics of the Antitextual Gesture." In Contours of the Theatrical Avant-garde: Performance and Textuality, edited by James M. Harding, 79-95. Ann Arbor: University of Michigan Press, 2000.

John Hill, The Actor: A Treatise on the Art of Playacting: Interspersed with Theatrical Anecdotes, Critical Remarks on Plays and Occasional Observations on Audiences (London: R. Griffiths, 1750)

Henry Siddons, Practical Illustrations of Rhetorical Gesture and Action; Adapted to the English Drama: From a Work on the Subject by M. Engel, Member of the Royal Academy of Berlin (London: Sherwood, Neely and Jones, 1822)

David Thomas, "The 1737 Licensing Act and its Impact," The Oxford Handbook of the Georgian Theatre, 1737-1832, ed. Julia Swindells and David Francis Taylor (Oxford: Oxford University Press, 2014), 101-102.

Claudio Vicentini, Theory of Acting: From Antiquity to the Eighteenth Century (Napoli: Acting Archives, 2012)

Shearer West, The Image of the Actor: Verbal and Visual Representation in the Age of Garrick and Kemble (New York: St. Martin's Press, 1991)

# On the Archaic and the Avant-Garde

A NOTE FROM DR. DICK PRICEY

You hold in your hands a ridiculous document, and yet one we hope will be of lasting historical import. Aping the form of a two hundred year old, largely forgotten illustrated acting treatise, we have sought to document a community of performers who we feel define the cutting edge of performance in contemporary theater. One could easily question the wisdom of trading in so archaic a form whilst striving for longevity. So allow me to start you off with a question: do we, in our embrace of the archaic, imply that our own work and those of the artists here represented will, like the original, become obsolete—a trace of a culture familiar in form, but ultimately illegible to our sensibilities?

Perhaps. But let's approach this with some perspective. For in our impending obsolescence there may be some call for exaltation. And not only from our detractors.

This project marks the end of this company's sixteen year journey into the archaic and the arcane. For these many years, we at the National Theater of the United States of America have worked collaboratively and compulsively, mining the history of American entertainment culture to make work that draws from the past even as it expresses contemporary concerns. Drawing from a multitude of theatrical styles, performance genres and other forms of art and media, we have often mashed these forms together, in an attempt to forge from them, in each project, a new aesthetic universe, a fully realized theatrical otherworld.

From such wide ranging phenomena as 19th century parlor theatricals, amusement park rides, zombie films, Chautauquas and self-empowerment seminars, we have embraced a kind of historical eclecticism, and in doing so have spurred reactions ranging from admiration to ire, from astonishment to eye-rolling, none of which we mind.

But through it all, one question has hounded us, and more so from within our organization than without. And that question is this: what makes our work experimental? What, with our proscenium stages and our costumes and our "characters" and our hidden technologies... what exactly is our claim to the status of the avant-garde? The answer to this question, I think, lies in a connection I'd like to draw between the archaic and the avant-garde.

As it is often noted, "avant-garde" is a term drawn from military parlance. It describes those battalions on the front lines who drive relentlessly forward in an unyielding attempt to establish new frontiers in the theatre of war. Implied in its metaphorical usage is a spirit of hope, ingenuity, selfless determination and belief that the causes for which we fight are worth all of that carnage, sacrifice and hard work—if only one of us can break through and breach new ground. And, indeed, from these bloodiest of trenches, heroes arise, individuals who through wit, grit and luck come to define for us, in their moment of triumph, the spirit of their age.

In the meantime, time moves only and forever forward. And while our heroes remain celebrated as symbols of our collective progress, and while the core values that drive them may never cease to hold true, in their historicization, in their transformation from blood and bone to pure symbol, these heroes are abstracted from their actual work. Indeed, even as they hover as gods above us, the gestures and actions that brought them to glory, with time, come to seem curious and quaint. Even as their tools remain identifiable as such, we often no longer conceive of how they functioned in their historical context. Made strange by the passage of time, these objects become signifiers of what once was, without ever the *what* that once was being known. In essence, they become archaic. And, in that, they become *absurd.*

The archaic then becomes us. The theater of the absurd, that avant-garde of the 1920s and 30s, celebrated, with no little morbidity, the futility of human existence as the world recoiled in horror from the first global war. But they did not do so without love for that world. Rather, they mocked it in all of its perversity in a petulant *refusal* to stop living, in an embrace of the life that would not leave them, even as logic of the world seemed to have left them behind. The late Herbert Blau is often cited for his observation that the power of live performance resides in the dialectic between a text or a character that persists across time and the actor performing it who is literally "dying in front of your eyes."

In precisely this spirit, we embrace the archaic in the acknowledgement of the absurdity of our historical condition. We acknowledge the pomposity of our desires, of our striving for historical relevance. We acknowledge the flailing futility of our gestures in the scope of geological time. We acknowledge those gestures, but we do not mock them. Rather, we celebrate them, as we celebrate our own impermanence. For in them is a reminder that the job of the avant-garde is not to set new foundations, but to dig the trenches that may occasion their arrival and then to move on. Should another come upon those trenches and fill them with concrete, then perhaps an edifice will be built and our legacy will persist, if only for a spell.

For it is these gestures that keep us alive, that remind us, even in the face of geological time, that we must live, that we must strive and that, in our striving, we are not alone. And so we celebrate the archaic in the acknowledgement that we are all fools whose truths may endure even as we most assuredly will be turned to dust.

Dr. Dick Pricey is an esteemed performacist and educateur who has been a leading voice for the NTUSA since its inception. From 2002 to 2004 he was head of the controversial James Stanley School of Very Much Acting where he developed his quantitative approach to the theater arts guided by the maxim: "How much acting should one do? Very much!" While Mr. Stanley has himself disavowed the school and its methods, that school has without a doubt produced some of the loudest and fastest theatrical performers of our generation.

# *Practical Illustrations*

Fig. 1

# Devotion

*as portrayed by Edgar Oliver*

A devoted shape is characterized by folding. When we devote ourselves we bow and crumple. To achieve Devotion, think of the curling of each small part, of the body and of the clothing, of the hair. But significantly, Devotion does not curl in the way a newspaper curls when it is burnt. It maintains eye contact with the adored object, in the air, slightly off-stage. The face lifts up to receive its reward.

Devotion, you'll apprehend, is not soggy. It retains its crispness. Crisp without being brittle. It is not over-stoic—it betrays its tenderness around the eyes and mouth. Imagine a tender folding, like folding new washed sheets that have dried in the sun. Your lover's sheets, or the sheets of a very nice child.

Fig. 2

# Enthusiasm

*as portrayed by Nikki Calonge*

It's simplest to imagine surprises: a gift, or gift opening. Perhaps hugs at the airport, or at a party.

A more advanced way is to remember flying. As an actor you needn't make anything up. You can just look out the window and imagine being outside of the window. Outside the window you are in the air and looking down, without danger, just joy of seeing. Think of the moment after a leap up, a moment of hanging in the air. Consider the newness of that feeling, the delight.

Not only delight, enthusiasm is a kind of mad fervor: enthusiasm abandons. The body loses its government. Strange things leap out of the mouth: pearls, frogs, poems, prophesies.

But enthusiasm also has its rigor, finds its source in the eyes. Open the eyes and the body opens. The chest broadens and rises.

Enthusiasm, most advanced: make a fire on your own.

Fig. 3

# Brotherly Love

*as portrayed by Joe Silovsky and Stanley the Robot*

Brotherly Love could be otherwise described as a form of fraternal self-confidence. Actors seeking to portray Brotherly Love must relax, releasing their spines and their hydraulics. The actors might imagine backyard nature, or sharing a can of beer in the gloaming, with crickets.

A tender, fraternal attention is nurtured here, in the turn of the neck. A care for your fellow's mood resides in the angle of the reassuring arm. The actors may choose to think of fishing in a silence punctuated only by splashing and the occasional utterance—"Welp..."

Or other scenarios. Lying in a hammock with legs intertwined. Patting each other's backs. Or after the battle, tending to wounds. In all, a species of contentment, as expressed in a loose posture and a gentle touch.

Fig. 4

# Distraction and Persuasion

*as portrayed by Jenn Harris and Matt Wilkas*

Distraction and Persuasion do not intersect. Observe their negative space. Their tension is that of the glass of milk that has spilt and the small fly that circles it.

The actors portraying Distraction and Persuasion must feint and thrust. While it might seem that this relationship is uneven, that one is doing all of the feinting, upon studying these positions you will soon see that there is aggression in feinting. Distraction can conceal, and Persuasion can be subject.

In the positions of Distraction and Persuasion these thoughts may come, unbidden, to the actors:

DISTRACTION: Was there a bug in here?

PERSUASION: It was a very small spaceship.

DISTRACTION: Or the wind changed?

PERSUASION: With a small man. Maybe it was more like a small blimp. But I saw the man. He looked at me. A tiny red scarf. Then his eye.

DISTRACTION: What are we having for lunch?

PERSUASION: He had a message for us. For you. He said: Open a savings account.

DISTRACTION: I once had a sandwich....

PERSUASION: He said: Start a home business, you know, something you can do on the side.

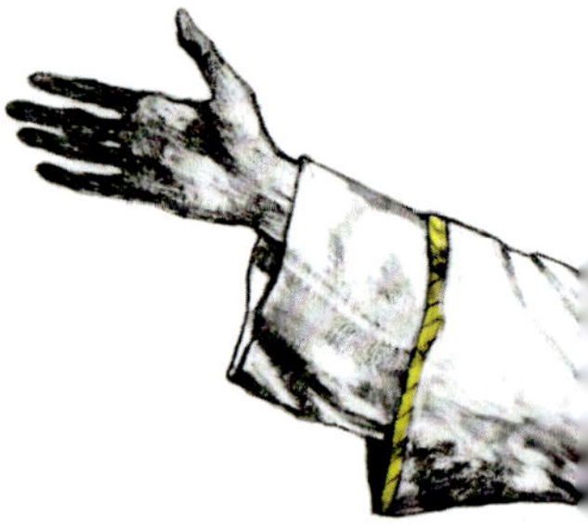

Fig. 5

# Tranquil Joy

*as portrayed by Kate Valk*

Tranquil Joy expands. A lightness in all of the parts of the body, lifting up and opening out. A weight released. A bubble, or rather, a spanner. No longer cringing from the blow. Beatitude.

Where did the weight go? Evaporated in air. Some bodies manifest joy in rictus, in a tense squeezing—but this is a misleading corporeal joy, tending to result in the False Gesture. Tranquil Joy has a lightness, holding itself lightly. In Joy of all forms there is forgetfulness of the body. A slight smile, showing teeth. The body creates space for itself, space between fingers, between the chin and the chest. The body is long, but not in tension. The body is open and not stiff.

This is one of the graceful positions.

Fig. 6

# False Gesture No. 1

*as portrayed by Magin Schantz*

Memorize this, the False Gesture:

> *"The charm resulting from it will be only for the eyes; the spirit will find there no enjoyment and the heart will still continue void and vacant."*
>
> —Siddons, Letter XXVII

Suppose an actor, splaying but not planting her legs, begins to indicate a point in the distance. Let us say in this case it is a Basket of Eggs in the City of Rome. This fact exists only in the mind of the actor, it is not communicated, unless someone has had the foresight to make a placard (or series of placards) indicating this state of affairs.

Suppose the actor, mid-gesture, is struck by another thought (which we cannot know) —a thought that results in a presentation of the hand, and an unseemly tilt to the neck. We will naturally wonder: What is meant? Forced to answer this in examining the length of the hair, the choice in wardrobe, the turn of the foot, we grow mutinous. How are we to know about the eggs? How are we to know about the meaning of the eggs?

A blameless basket of eggs, gingerly pushed onstage from the wings, has more figurative power. How are we to know that the cupped hand, in the mind of the actor, holds, perhaps, a single egg.

The author of the False Gesture, flailing, ends in pantomime or worse. Ends in miming the wrong things. The author of the play has written a line about "opening a can of worms." The actor mimes the worms.

But. Is there not pleasure in this falseness? As in shopping for false eyelashes? As if indicating artificial snow?

Fig. 7

# Painful Recollection

*as portrayed by David Patrick Kelly*

Observe the hand: raised as if to ward off some haze or vapor of Painful Recollection. The brow creased, the eyes mostly closed, the bending of the spine: the curl. Observe the tension in the hands, a slight clenching. The stance is not quite a stagger but he isn't steady on his pins—tension in his belly, making his back arch. He is bracing himself. The internal state becomes external.

Experts claim that Painful Recollection is the seat—the wellspring—of all acting. For this reason we present:

## USEFUL EXERCISES

### FOR NOVICES

1. Contract the muscles of the belly as if warding off a kick.
2. As if warding off a snake.
3. As if pushing against a strong wind. Remember to do something with your hands. Are you holding something?

### FOR THE ADVANCED STUDENT

A. Once when we were very young, we paused in the middle of enjoying a glass of milk—a bee buzzed. All at once we were forcefully brought to mind of the first bee sting that laid us low. Remember the hot, then the cool of the parents' bedroom. The screaming. Oh how pitiful it was, and how small we were, how unable to understand the cruel pain of bees.

B. Remembering when I, hopeful, hands full of flowers, came skipping along to meet my beloved. When was it? Summertime? Near to darkness, by the gate. She was smoking a corncob pipe, with an air of secrecy. The moments walking up. It was still light, I saw her and she saw me, the air was clear. We were far from each other and prudently waited to hail one another. But then, with perhaps fifty feet to go, seeing the neighbor boy swoop in, bearing his own worse flowers, smiling and leaning in to kiss her. And in that moment: the sky darkening and I, walking closer and closer, raising my hand to hail her. And in that moment, before I could loose those words, so carefully composed, seeing them laugh, clasp hands and retire into the house. Afterwards, I waited in the darkness, at the edge of a pool of weak light from the porch. I didn't knock. I laid the flowers on the step and turned around, towards home.

### FOR TRAINED EXPERTS

The most advanced advice that can be given is that all recollection is painful. Even the happiest fancies of youth can be used to provoke appropriately painful recollections if you contextualize them in thinking of the disappointments of age. Or, if you are not yet disappointed, perhaps by meditating on the future and the potential for grimness it offers.

Fig. 8

# Indulgence

*as portrayed by Radiohole*

Profusion of bodies, of bottles, of wieners. Truly, these are carcasses. The obscuring of the face makes the body more visible, the hotdogs more prominent.

But in all this, centrally, a tube. Indulgence is a pose that requires things to be indulged in, tubes and bottles to speed the act. The figure in the center sucks the breath from the figure at right. It grabs the crotch of the wiener-laden figure on the left. It has covered itself with a mask of papers, is this, then, the god?

For in such a group picture, one searches for the figure who could be called most indulgent.

Perhaps it is the figure on the floor, in underwear and capelet, with an open mouth waiting for fluids and wieners. Indulgence closes its eyes, ready to be satiated by whatever falls into its open mouth.

Fig. 9

# Horror

*as portrayed by Juliana Francis Kelly*

Horror beholds, but it unfolds in the mind. Horror is intimate. It is a gesture of realization rather than of reacting to a present threat. And yet the gesticulations of Horror are large, they open up. The attitude of the head—please note—the head wants to turn away but the face must look—the face must face.

Horror does not cringe. It is a species of inviting gesture. Horror animates the upper body (we have yet to see horrified legs and ankles dancing, though we'll admit it may not be impossible). Horror turns away and asks others to be horrified. Horror asks us to behold. Behold the hand on the right, wrist pressing forehead. The hand wants to cover the face but—no—it cannot. In horror, the hands must realize that they are useless.

And if Terror reacts to a threat—perhaps a giant bird that swoops down on your village to pluck the children up—then Horror is when we are held rapt by a sight—it is finding an unlabeled shoebox in the bottom of your closet, and opening it. The village must know what you see—that the box contains the bones of those children.

Fig. 10

# Despondency

*as portrayed by Ilan Bachrach*

> *"For interior operations execute themselves proportionably better as they are the less troubled by the exterior impressions of the senses ... For this reason, love, sorrow and chagrin, as well as all of the reflective passions, delight in the silent obscurity of groves. The owl is the attribute of the Goddess of Wisdom, because an inhabitant of the deserts: he makes his watch in the stillness and the obscurity of the night."*
>
> —Siddons, Letter IX

All that keeps the body up is the trunk—the trunk must do a lot of work.

All other organs quietly wilt. A solitary position: we interrupt the actor in his privacy. We sense thinking. But he seems not to sense what we privately suspect, or to care.

In former times, we could have said "He's lost in a brown study." We'd say it if, on entering a room, we chanced on this figure, ruminating and forlorn. We'd say it to gently chide him, to bring him back to his senses. He might resent us.

In Despondency, the chair must do a lot of work, sorrow and lassitude infect the limbs. He lost his owl, named Goddess. The owl is happy, probably, but the slumping figure cannot appreciate that now. He cannot even appreciate a grove—or a desert—or his furniture—or Boston.

Boston must do a lot of work, the tragedy of Boston, unspoken but always known.

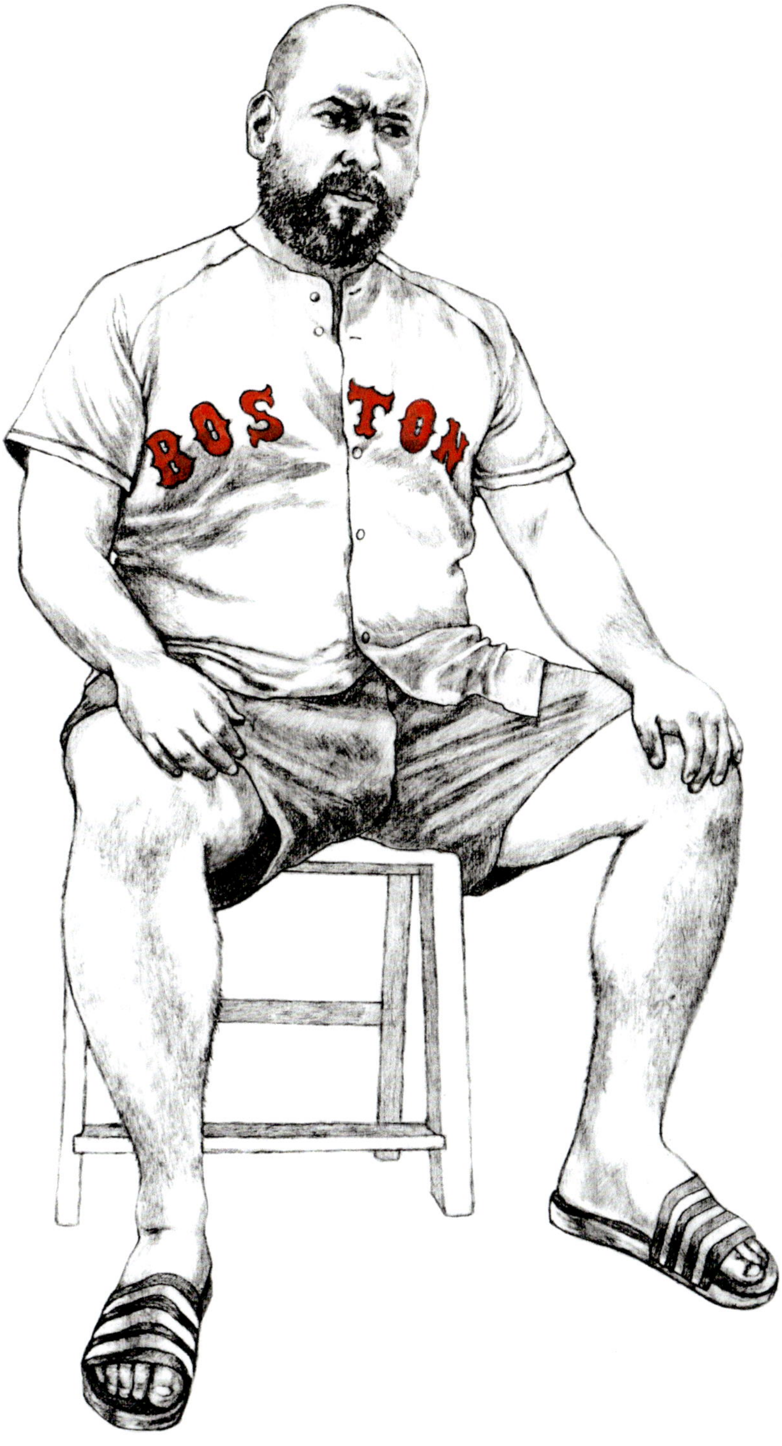
BOSTON

Fig. 11

# Despair

*as portrayed by Okwui Okpokwasili*

Despair is shaped by absence.

The figure hollows out, allows the exoskeleton of the draperies to make shapes. The body of Despair is aware of the vanity of shapes.

The left hand almost closes on something. It curves. It could hold the hand of a child, a sword or a sandwich. It doesn't.

Despair hoods and shrouds itself. A forward gaze, a listless eye, limpness in the limbs and in the garment. Despair resigns, it is fixed, it fails to notice cold or bees or lights.

Despair, resplendent in its patience, is aware that the ship is burning in the distance, offstage. Perhaps the ship's burning has not been confirmed—a ship is burning in the mind. Perhaps the ship is in full view, with sails, with sailors, with a topless mermaid on the prow. That is to say, cheerful. But the mind is occupied with the possibility of the ship burning.

Once thought, the word burning never subsides, voiding out the ship: uncashable check.

Even so. We can see the toes of Despair. Even so: we can think: "Within Despair there is a Hope, the toes peeking out."

Fig. 12

# Triumph

*as portrayed by Aleta and Jim Findlay*

Do you know how Athena came out of Zeus's forehead?

The story is that Athena's mother Metis got into some sort of fight with Zeus, and then in the heat of the fight Zeus ate Metis. Metis had her baby while trapped in Zeus's forehead. This baby was Athena, who trained for years to be strong enough to get out of that godly skull.

Zeus got a lot of headaches.

Finally, Zeus asked Haephestus, Ares and also some other god to help him ease his pain, so they broke open his skull. What did they break it open with? A golden axe.

Athena sprang out in Triumph.

Notice the straight torso of the triumphant, the arm reaching higher, and the other hand pushing the head of the opponent down.

The triumphant feels the Triumph as a tension in the legs—it is slippery to balance on the head of the vanquished.

The triumphed over feels Triumph in the neck, while it is being trampled.

It would be difficult to portray Triumph without a person to be triumphed over. It wouldn't be as sweet if the triumphant one weren't seemingly outmatched. Triumph can and should show its teeth. The word is close to trumpet, because trumpets are always playing, somehow and somewhere. Triumph is an internal sound of trumpets as you step on some(one). Triumph makes stilts out of the skulls of those it triumphs over. Every Triumph makes you a skull-head taller, because you are stepping on all of the skulls at once. An interesting problem is posed—how to translate this gesture into scenes of solo Triumph. It's all in the imagining, shoes made of skulls. This is an explicitly allegorical pose. It is good for portraying the young triumphing over their forefathers, or any time a small girl triumphs over a huge man.

Fig. 13

# Hopeless Love

*as portrayed by Black Eyed Susan*

The skull will crack. Protect it, keep it closed with gentle pressure. The hope kept it sutured, its flight makes a fissure. Look up and away.

This is a gesture that is very convenient for the theater. An actor can't always be howling. You'd think that hopeless love might be something that reaches out, that trails its fingers on the table or in the grasses at the edge of a pond. But do these things and you will only convey distraction. For surely hopeless love is not limp, it is instead knotted, braided tight. The hair is braided and the muscles. It can't untwist.

Hopeless Love exists also in the brow. It curdles there.

Fig. 14

# Astonishment

*as portrayed by Saori Tsukada*

> *"Astonishment, like thought, stops suddenly short when an object of interest presents itself unexpectedly to the view."*
>
> —Siddons, Letter X

Think about inhaling the air in the moment of Astonishment, hold it there in your lungs.

That may be all you need to think of.

Or think of your body as the bag of a vacuum. The vacuum sucks up the air. How to hold it there? How to make a shape from the air inside? The shape of the air is the shape of the expression Astonishment. You'll feel it in your core muscles, and everything will appear to radiate from that. But what you are truly sucking up and holding is not air, it is the audience.

This practice is good for any astonishing moment. It also can be used to fool someone.

Fig. 15

# Fashionable Impudence

*as portrayed by Ean Sheehy*

The Incroyable in empire France shocked the populace with his high collar, his pink-striped vest and with the improbable ratio of his waist to his shoulders—produced by tight lacing and padding. His impudence manifested in his lack of function—his clothes were good only for surprising people in the park. People said: "How Dare He?" They also said "He looks stupid." But they said these things to disguise the fact that they were deeply terrified by what Fashionable Impudence points to—that there is no reason anyone has to be any particular way at all.

The most impudent pose is a nonsensical one. Who would ride a vespa thus? It is a nonsense that invokes power, or the appearance of power—he can ride a vespa thus because he can afford not to care about the discomfort of riding on the vespa thus. Fashionable Impudence can be a kind of protest, fashioning nonsense resistance as political resistance. What is he protesting? Comfort? Physics? It is a Pose that can take many forms. We could say the Fashionable Impudence of the Incroyables made everyone else in France very uncomfortable by enacting an acceleration of the ridiculousness of the fashions they participated in—a kind of nihilistic fashion gamesmanship. That's an exciting way to think about it, though these guys were probably just bored rich guys who wanted to look cool.

*

To obtain this attitude you must look out and see a bunch of losers who wish they were you…

Losers who are watching you.

And you really don't have time to deal with their attention.

But you're used to being watched all the time. Everybody's always looking at you. They may look, as long as they don't bother you.

You have to become very comfortable with your own superiority… you have to know that you've just come from some sort of very luxurious very sensual very lazy encounter.

First, you relax. Because everything has already been accomplished there's no effort to make, it's all completely natural. Not only that, you're also somewhat exhausted from your sybaritic excesses: drinking, sex, eating, massages.

Your wrists feel loose, slack. Your chin tilts.

Fashionable Impudence is the pose of an unobtainable lover, or an upper-class character who is young and cruel.

This pose is good for self-esteem.

Fig. 16

# Rivalry

*as portrayed by Ari Fliakos and Scott Shepherd*

To portray Rivalry, you need two actors. The actors must be must be in opposition to and engaged with each other at the same time. An actor might choose to display his manly chest. An actor might consider the relative hostility of the tilt of the head. The actors might decide to look at each other a little bit, out of the corners of the eyes. The actors might fill up each other's space provokingly without acknowledging this.

The actor on the right, Mr. Scott Shepherd, gazes directly at the audience, as if to communicate to his rival, Mr. Ari Fliakos, that he is beneath notice.

A shortcut to Rivalry:

It's like this, imagine cops. There's one cop who really wants to be a good cop. Or rather, he thinks he's the greatest cop because he's been doing cop stuff for so long. And then his partner, a different kind of guy, a guy with sunglasses, probably, is like: "I don't even like cops! I'm just doing this cop stuff because I'm amazing. But I actually don't care."

That's the kind of Rivalry you might envision.

Fig. 17

# Pride

*as portrayed by Mikéah Jennings*

> *"Does any one admire the charms and beauty of his own figure, or the activity and grace of his movements; then the soft smile of internal contentment, the vivacity of soul, the gaiety of gesture remain; he leaps, runs, sings—a thousand attitudes succeed, that he may be able to look at and admire himself under several points of view."*
>
> —Siddons, Letter XXVII

Pride looks forward with candor. Pride shows off his plumage. No bashfulness, no shrinking. The chest points up, as in "puffs up his chest." Where does Pride come from? All sorts of places, but it can be provoked by something as simple as a fancy shirt.

This actor is demonstrating warranted Pride—unwarranted Pride would exaggerate details, such as the choice of a shirt, in order to give the audience a sense of superiority to the actor's mumming. Warranted pride keeps pride rightfully placed, evident in the dignified body and carriage of the actor as he wears the bejeweled shirt. Unwarranted pride (or, more extremely, "Conceit") would show the spectator that the actor's pride in his fancy, dopey shirt misplaced.

A true portrayal of Pride communicates to us that the shirt is fancy and cool, and that the actor is beautiful, overriding any objective quibbles the spectator might have.

Could we call Pride the absence of shame? Or the certainty of one's own beauty and dignity? It is a beautiful gesture, when the audience is allowed to understand that it is warranted.

Fig. 18

# Loftiness

*as portrayed by Lucy Taylor*

Chin up, a tilted chin, aim cloudsward. Elongate the neck, even if you were told that your neck is "not exactly swanlike." Elongate it anyway to be a swan, the loftiest of the birds. To be lofty is to be high minded—not stuck up, but elevated. Notice the brows are highbrow, an archness and a gentle amusement is appropriate to loftiness.

Loftiness can be simple, so simple. It can wear simple clothes. It needs no diamond. It keeps up, up tall like a ballet dancer, it gestures enigmatically with the hands.

The classic advice of dance teachers—release the tension in your shoulders. Can you remember this in your body? The shoulders want to hunch and the neck! Well, the neck wants to unswan. To be lofty you have to elongate your neck and even your whole spine, which should feel really pleasant. Relaxing. You spend most of your time with bad posture, and this is your opportunity to straighten up and open out your shoulders and feel tall.

It's different from Pride.

We might see Pride as an imposing statue, hard and weighty, supported by earth. Loftiness isn't Pride, because it relaxes in its altitude. We find ballet dancers to be lofty because they can move like little wooden bead puppet heads suspended by wires while their bodies describe smooth shapes. The muscular motion somehow emanates directly from the forehead, as if the brain were really the engine. The Loftiness of the ballet supports this dear fantasy of body hierarchy.

Loftiness perches. It has purchase on air. It balances ballet-like, recalling childhood technique. The child who trains as a ballet dancer goes into graceful, lofty poses with its ungraceful body. The pose of Loftiness does something to your body but it also does something to the way you're feeling, your poise and sense of stillness. But when you are playing somebody who conceives of themselves as lofty, above other people to the point of Conceit, this kind of character is always secretly more earthly, more troubled and more prone to fault than she believes herself to be.

The practice of Loftiness can be good on two levels—it can be good for allowing you to feel those cloudsward feelings of being somehow above earthly cares, but it can also be good to perceive that there is a floor in it and that if you are so high above you can miss out on reality.

Fig. 19

# Conceit

*as portrayed by Sibyl Kempson*

Conceit aims up, and is careful as a cat of its limbs and extremities.

You must compare Conceit with Pride to appreciate the subtleties of the gesture. You will see similarities. Both are emboldened by fancy paisley-figured shirts. While Pride looks out with candor, however, Conceit looks away with a delicate wrinkling of the face, as if sucking the juice of the kumquat.

Conceit is, of course, artificial—is a kind of manufactured pride. It is a degraded copy of pride. That's how we understand it. Or maybe that Pride is of the body and Conceit is intellectual. It is one of those mannered exaggerations that unwarranted pride can pervert and distort into.

Conceit does not want to see you. It delicately pinches its glasses. The motion derives from the chin. The body holds something within, carefully. As if the body is a display case for a treasure—some crown or wand, something precious and obscure. Or maybe more like a vial of powdered rhinoceros horn, an eyedropper-full of basilisk milk. Something rare that could get used up too quickly.

Conceit holds tension in the arms, the upper arms, the shoulders, the thigh, and even in the face and neck. The tension suffuses the body. Even so, it is one of the graceful positions. It is also one of the upward positions.

Fig. 20

# Menace

*as portrayed by Paul Lazar*

To achieve Menace the actor must conjure an old power, maybe something from the seventeenth or eighteenth century. Your body must become aristocratic in order to reflect hierarchical power structures. Your body must tell you that you're somewhere in that hierarchy. It is a fierce hierarchy, and unsentimental: either you are being destroyed from above or you are destroying someone below. You must be the destroyer.

Read the diaries of Samuel Pepys, you will see: Pepys is a civilized and sophisticated guy, but he'll go and watch people being hung in whatever that park is in the center of London. In the seventeenth and eighteenth centuries there was a much higher tolerance for what we would now consider to be unacceptably brutal. That's a very, very hot and lively thing to be plugged into, and though it's completely off limits, to portray Menace we must acknowledge that we all have completely homicidal impulses within us.

This embodiment of Menace starts from the turn out of the hips. These days we might ascribe an effete quality to that kind of turn out, but this is an underestimation of its ruthlessness.

The portrayal of Menace needs a kind of aggressive openness, push your chest out more. You must be overt with your intentions and unsubtle. Even in times where being unsubtle seems ill-advised, it can be liberating and even a good idea, in terms of acting.

Menace enacts violence without touching. It is a violence of fixed gazes, of hand-clenches and chin-tilts. To enact Menace, you may need to recall being menaced: you might access Menace by recalling moments when strangers threatened to punch you. The effect this threat can have on the body is to teach it to narrow, to teach your body to close off the kinesphere for the purpose of not entangling with punchers. Then, once the menacing moment is embodied, you have to turn it out the opposite way. Reverse it by opening the shoulders and stepping in to an aggressive forward motion. It may feel good to inhabit a menacing character's physicality. It may feel scary as your desire-to-menace rushes in.

Fig. 21

# Mirth

*as portrayed by Jess Barbagallo*

You could begin by thinking of things that provoke Mirth—communist propaganda posters of happy babies. Or some sort of foreign film that was like a caper—where you are riding in the sidecar but somehow driving. That's right, all the abandon of the sidecar with the agency of driving the bike!

You could begin by thinking in shapes. Think about your body as made up of a series of shapes that communicate things. You could begin with an attempt at smiling in your forearms. Consider the motion of cheering, of cheering for yourself or cheering for other people—all the people collecting, getting excited about all the soccer games and the feeling of wanting to leap to your foot or feet and raise your arm in a cheer. Where does that come from?

You may find that portraying Mirth turns into real mirth—the gesture gives the feeling. When you start to smile and move it shakes something in you and that shaking is like laughing, can produce the effect of laughing. Even if you are bummed in your day-to-day there are contortions of the body that will alter your state of mind. Even if you don't like being at parties, for instance, try holding up a stein of beer in a jovial fashion. That could be a useful way to be in that scene, mirthfully, without necessarily feeling it.

"What do you do if you're not feeling it?" is a sensible question to ask if you're a student who is being taught about authenticity. But the answer is, frustratingly: "Oh you just fake it."

Faking is of the theater. The theater happens because the actors and the audience are all in the room together: there's nothing wrong with being illustrative, in telling stories with your body. That might make you feel cheeseball, but that is why you're there.

Fig 22

# Idiotism

*as portrayed by Mike Iveson and Ben Williams*

> *"...the head, which, not being properly placed on the neck, sinks upon the bosom; the open lip, which draws down the chin with its natural weight; the eyes of which the pupils are almost obscured by the lids; the knees bending out, and the feet turned in... One cannot avoid acknowledging a soft soul and an idle mind, unsusceptible of any attention, uninfluenced by any interest, which is never thoroughly awake, and does not possess the feeble energy which is necessary to give the tension requisite for the muscles and for the proper support of the body. An attitude so full of nullity, so dead and inanimate, can only belong to the extremity of mournful imbecility, or the effects of the most contemptible idleness."*
>
> —Siddons, Letter VIII

Idiotism does not imagine, it is one of the vapid positions. Idiotism is not fantasy based it's experience based. It's experiential. Some people work from the outside in and some people work from the inside out. The portrayal of Idiotism you see here requires two actors, one to embody the slackness and vacancy of Idiotism, and one to mimic this slackness because it seems like that's what people are doing now. Many people are on the edge of Idiotism at any hour of any day.

Idiotism is neck-work-based. The neck must swallow the head, contract like a recalcitrant turtle. In general, if you are not portraying Idiotism, you must avoid this practice of contraction—recall that spinal elongation is the hallmark of the graceful position (see Tranquil Joy, Loftiness). While Idiotism is neck-based, it is not neck-centric: you will also want to feel Idiotism in your extremities: your hands, also in your mouth, possibly your nose.

This is a gesture that many find useful in daily life, particularly in manipulative contexts, like copy-editing. Idiotism is a great cloak to throw on, because then you can turn around and pop out some big vocab words and nobody knows what's going on.

Fig. 23

# Agility

*as portrayed by Johanna Meyer*

To demonstrate Agility is to seem to scoff at weight, all the while managing it carefully.

Agility knows its own weightiness and how to lift up out of it. Recall again the ballet, which aims to get up off the ground: this is supposed to be better than being connected to the ground. You need to find the lift or carriage in your trunk, the ease up through your hip joints. You need to find momentum, which helps propel you from the ground and back to it, then away from it again.

Could you be this agile, young actor? You have a better chance if you are young. Agility is an expression of physical skill. Is there a physical skill you can express?

Siddons writes in Letter III that "feats of Agility, perilous leaps and jumps are beneath the dignity of even a legitimate pantomime, which represents action, and whose object is to incite both interest and attention." This is because Agility in excess refers only to the body of the performer "the individual alone," and does not do the social work of communicating the meaning of the drama.

These feats do communicate pleasure and liveliness, which is often enough to please the audience.

Fig. 24

# Anger

*as portrayed by Matt Kalman*

Anger brings the butt to the ground, raises the fist.

Anger opens up, holds the body open like the stick holding an alligator's jaws apart in the cartoons. Anger can be provoked by many things, a foe, a broken tea pot, a bee. But the true manifestation of anger is anger at the gods, it goes heavenward. It is open to cursing, anger allows an odd openness to being cursed, a kind of daring—dare the gods to strike me down, my cares and cautions are burnt away in the heat of my wrath.

*

Normandy: Did you feel tension in any particular part of your body?

Matt: Ahh yeah. All over. It's a pretty tense gesture.

Fig. 25

# Sublime Adoration

*as portrayed by Maxwell Cosmo Cramer*

> *"…you will remark that the body imitates the expansion of the soul, whilst seeking to seize on a grand object, with which all its representative forces appear to be replete. The mouth and eyes are open, the eyebrows are slightly drawn upwards, the arms are certainly nearer the body than in quick and animated desire, yet they are still somewhat extended; in other respects, the body and the traits of the countenance are in repose."*
>
> —Siddons, Letter X

This is a kind of worship of beauty, a delicate and ethereal gesture. A supplicating gesture—the sublime is akin to awe. Imagine these objects of awe: Clouds, Baby, Falling, Teddy Bear, Water Fall, Bodies of Water, Heavenly Bodies.

Or you could take a different tack: imagine awe-ful experiences as depicted in Home Alone 2: Fear, Childhood Celebrity, Macaulay Culkin, Hotels, Hotel Staff, Service, Emotional Labor.

You must release the desire to see yourself—merely maintain a self awareness, a sense of abandon. Listen closely and proceed intuitively. You will feel a strain in your shoulders, your back and arms, your core, especially when you recline.

Sometimes it will feel more affected, and sometimes less affected. It can be embodied with varying degrees of energy and can be quite simple.

Always there will be a feeling of simultaneous tension but also a release, a heightened state that is at once kind of frightening but also kind of inspiring and is also kind of synonymous with the event of performing.

Sublime Adoration recalls the moment of a direct kind of engagement with the audience, the moment where the actor contemplates the audience, is receptive to being watched.

It is necessary in Shakespeare and Greek tragedy, also in Transformers. You can see it in the posters.

Fig. 26

# False Gesture No. 2

*as portrayed by Faye Driscoll*

> *"You have doubtless forgotten the contents of many of my former letters since you ask ... A man who should attempt to copy the manners of a sailor begging in the street might hit off his tone, his look, and his gesture, but the want of the wooden leg would still render the painting deficient."*
>
> —Siddons, Letter XXV

Observe the limbs' angled disorder, the fist inserting into the mouth, the ambivalence of the spine.

This is a False Gesture that occurs in an interstitial space. Between one true gesture and the next, the meaning of the body becomes indeterminate, uncommitted. This is the fleeting moment of the failed experiment, a moment that doesn't help with the delineation of the character or the narrative. A moment where the body is overcome with self-consciousness, or where the movement doesn't complete a gesture—the movement becomes malformed or unnecessary. This is a moment where the body is unbalanced. Limbs go in different directions: face pointing one way, shoulders, arms going a different way at the same time.

The performer might ask "Does this look like anything?' and the watcher will respond: "No."

This is, of course, a place of freedom—a place where un-thought-of forms come into being. We must, perhaps, create many false gestures before we can create a gesture that means something new.

Will you still persist in gesturing falsely? Will you still clutch your hair, claw your face, look away from the audience without knowing what it means?

If you will, I leave you to your awkwardness.

Fig. 27

# Scorn

*as portrayed by Kourtney Rutherford*

> "*. . . those importunate and disagreeable ideas, which the mouth rejects, with the repetition of the word Pho, are in some measure likewise repulsed by a rapid agitation of the hand from one side to the other, as if we wished to chase away a teasing insect, which returns with double eagerness to the attack.*"
>
> —Siddons, Letter IX

The Scorn manifested here might be located chiefly in the sneer. It radiates from the sneer and goes into the hands, the stockinged legs, and even to the tip of the feather. Imagine passing some enemy or even ex-lover on the street, the shock in your bones and the muscles of your arms and shoulders, hot then cold.

But the Scorn does not start in the sneering lip, it begins with a tension in the muscles of the back of the neck, a tightening that causes the shoulders to move up protectively, seems to draw the face taut. It is only the most visible manifestation of the larger operation of the body's proud revulsion. A sneer is the closest we get to a growl in our polite circles.

Scorn ends cold, but it starts hot. It is a dousing of a hot passion and that's what can make it very cruel.

Scorn must be manifested in situations where honor or dignity is violated. It is a visible, pointed withdrawal. Scorn points at its object, as if to wither it by means of a laser, or some kind of x-ray beam that will help the spectator see the truth of the sorry object.

Fig. 28

# Hopefulness

*as portrayed by Aaron Landsman*

> *"Lastly hope, which only views bliss in the future, is not always free from fear; she can only then depict herself in one point of view; the traits of the visage must take an expression of desire, with a mixture of joy and fear."*
>
> —Siddons, Letter XXIII

Hopefulness inclines forward and up. It actually wants to lift off, to rise from the ground, but it tempers itself. Hopefulness is off-balance, though it carefully keeps a balancing toe near the ground, in case the hope should be disappointed. This gesture moves towards joy, but it is more tentative. Hopefulness is an awakening gesture—the fingers begin to spread out, and the arms begin to move up, as if to embrace the longed-for object. The mouth opens slightly—it wants to say: "Can this be true? You weren't dead at all? You were only in an Australian prison all of these years, and now you've come home?" Hopefulness denies doubt, but it doesn't forget doubt. The doubt is grounding.

For some, portraying Hopefulness requires zero technique.

For others, it will help to imagine a hope-striking object appearing in front of you, hovering, seemingly illuminated by occult rays. You will want to slow down. We move quickly to avoid our doubts, so that we may make choices before the doubt gets a hold on us. Slow down, and let the doubts catch up to you. Let them be the ropes that keep your balloon tethered until it's safe to ascend.

A gesture of Hopefulness is irresistible. It will draw people to you.

Fig. 29

# Death

*as portrayed by David Greenspan*

There are many ways to die, and any actor has had his fun in finding ways of dying. But to manifest the still point of Death is another thing entirely. Of course, I have known actors who began with Death, finding their first roles in the theater as the body on the slab and working up to the talking, moving parts from there.

Dying might be wracked, tense, with jagged breaths and wails. Death is prone, the hands relax, the muscles unknit, the jaw slackens. The chest expands, as if to begin a cracking open. The chest becomes an egg that the little soul pecks its way out of. To manifest Death, be an egg that can crack.

Make your eyes into little eggs, quail or robin eggs. The eyes become hardboiled eggs, the quickness congealed—cooked into matter. To manifest Death, stop being human and become an object for a time. It's safe because it's the theater.

The theater loves a death scene, any actor should have many ways to die pitifully, sweetly, angrily, stupidly (not on a chair though). But there is only one way to be Death convincingly, and that is to take a vacation from being a person.

Fig. 30

# Jealous Rage

*as portrayed by Pete Simpson*

The position of Jealous Rage exists between injury and aggression. There's something pathetic in this posture, but there's also something volatile, ready to attack.

If you wanted to train so that you could embody Jealous Rage, there's a Japanese business school you could attend. The school would make you go out on the street with your shame badges on and scream at the public. The shame badges are little banners hanging off of a belt, and you could lose them as you confronted all of the very shameful situations the school would put you in: like going out in public, like being at intersections and screaming and stuff. You would scream particular texts they had prepared for you to scream.

Perhaps this could help you to release your vapors.

Or, if you are an actor, you could also imagine yourself as a kid looking in the mirror, experimenting with your body and face. This could conjure a shock flash collage of a bunch of films and characters and bigger than life people, and what would be left when those images subsided would be a picture of you trying to figure out your alien face in front of a mirror at various ages of your life. You could imagine yourself, later, overcome by your own self-disgust on stage. Imagine yourself overwhelmed by your need to perform and disoriented by the things that got you to that place of having to perform. Jealous Rage thrives on surprise and confusion.

Jealous Rage creates a certain collapsing in your core—you have to take this massive muscle group and scrunch it to its smallest, most vulnerable size. That's what you do around a wound—if you're gut-shot you just collapse everything around it. This injured scrunching is the seat of Jealous Rage, and carries in it a kind of innocence. The surprise that you are the one who is in this predicament, fist-clenched, trou dropped, clutching a wig and hollering.

Fig. 31

# Fallen Greatness

*as portrayed by Kate Benson*

Fallen Greatness, when you are on the floor with a broken rocket, is an allegorical pose, a memento mori.

You could imagine being the chewing gum on the bottom of a shoe.

You could think about people you really admire feeling like things had once been more beautiful, feeling their feelings of disappointment in the way that the world turns out.

You have to have big ambition to really experience the fallen greatness. You could imagine a getting-arrested-after-winning-an-Oscar situation.

Or you might think about losing a lover, feeling so great—so good and so exciting—so excited when you're in love with someone. Then it ends and you just feel like: "ugh, that's over." Think about sex that doesn't work out, there's nothing to do here. Lie down, as in a rumpled bed, knocking over the rocket trophy.

But even while you are crunched up on the bed, you should make more space in your shoulders, which you habitually smoosh. Feel your awareness in your shoulder, the rotator cuffs and the little joints in there. Performing some kind of disappointment rather than actually just giving into the disappointment means you have to, like, make some kind of space there in your shoulders. Breathe, even though your hands might feel like they aren't quite sure what to do.

Perhaps you reject the idea that there is ever anything like perfection ever that we've fallen: you may consider Fallen Greatness to be more like our constant state.

Our constant state, disappointment, which is coping with all of the imperfections that exist. The world is a terrible place, though occasionally you can get access to how beautiful it is and how much the struggle people face is beautiful. It's important to remember that that's at the root of everything all the time, that you could lose whatever you have that's keeping the bubble of joy inflated.

When you're headed towards something wonderful, and everything seems to be lining up so that your own personal experience can be more exciting you ought to remember that that could change, and also that it is changing in the opposite direction for a lot of people. Don't feel so pleased with yourself. There is no doing things right, after all, there just is the luck of doing things today and then doing things a little better, a little more thoughtfully.

Fig. 32

# Folly

*as portrayed by Ayesha Jordan*

A grimace, a contortion. A sloppy reveal. Folly expresses thoughtlessness with the body. The Folly of expecting to be wearing underwear.

Folly is not a false gesture, it communicates.

What it communicates is dumbness, poor judgment, misplaced confidence in what turns out to have been a bad idea. Folly is the overconfidence that is haunted by ill fortune. Folly is felt in the tongue, shaping the mouth for the grimace. It is felt on the thighs, in the form of the breeze that caresses them as a result of their ill advised exposure. The cockiness of Folly is observable in the way the hips are pushed out and the spine curved back.

Folly: another one of the vapid positions. To perform Folly you must think you are something wonderful, while what you actually are is something ridiculous. This is a position accessible to most anyone at any time.

Fig. 33

# Sickness

*as portrayed by Brian Mendes*

You could, of course, remember the last time that you were violently sick, remember how you acted.

You could also consider your center of balance. How do you stand when your body at its most stable? How do you stand when your balance is precarious? Experiment with moving your center of balance back so your quadriceps take the weight rather than your skeleton. Imagine your skeleton is disintegrating, how do you keep your body in a roughly human form? Which bones go first? What do your muscles have to do to compensate, and what happens when they fail? Does the pelvis go first or does your left femur? Do you go all gumby? Or are you more like a shattering teacup? And while you decide how your skeleton rejoins the hungry dust on the floor, feel the pit of of your stomach as the fulcrum point, the tension radiating out.

The gesture of Sickness would be good to indicate that you are feeling ill. Would you do it in front of anyone? If you wanted to tell your wife or my friend that you were sick, would you dare? Perhaps this is a private gesture—a good gesture for when you're alone and you want to wallow in your sickness, just live in your Sickness for a moment, so that when somebody comes in the room you can regain your composure.

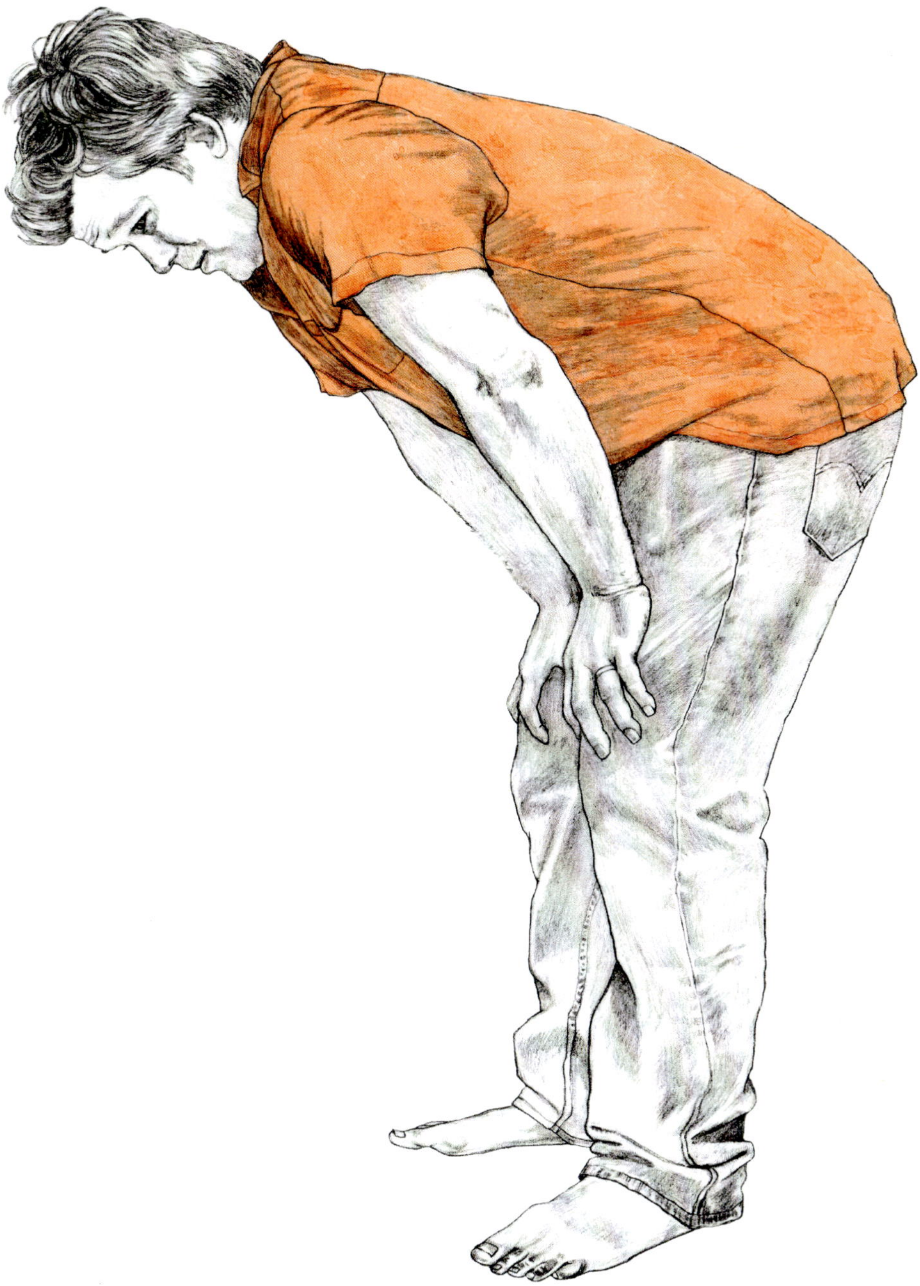

Fig. 34

# Doubt

*as portrayed by Kate Scelsa*

> *"In passing from one idea to the other, he loses himself in the labyrinths of doubt, which multiply in his mind a situation which could never be decent in an orator, encharged with the task of fixing and guiding the judgment of the public."*
>
> —Siddons, Letter XXXIII

We do not want to reveal our Doubt. Fingers extended, pressed over a worried mouth. No one shall know of our misgivings, but it is the gesture of hiding that reveals the misgiving. Doubt clings to itself. It masks an internal operation, a rearrangement of parts.

How do we make this process external?

It is in the fingers and the eyeballs, and especially the pointed toes. Find the Doubt in hands and eyes and feet. This portrayal of Doubt is quite intimate, portraying the moment when the doubt creeps in, and the confident presentation of self falters. Doubt is a horror that things are not what they seemed to be. Doubtful of the fish I ate, that looked so pink and healthy. Doubtful of the subtle friend, who said she would just borrow the car for an hour. Doubtful somewhere in a hedge maze, wondering whether to turn back and which way "back" is.

One might be tempted to portray spiritual or ideological Doubt on grander lines. But no, it looks the same. Protective and a little horrified.

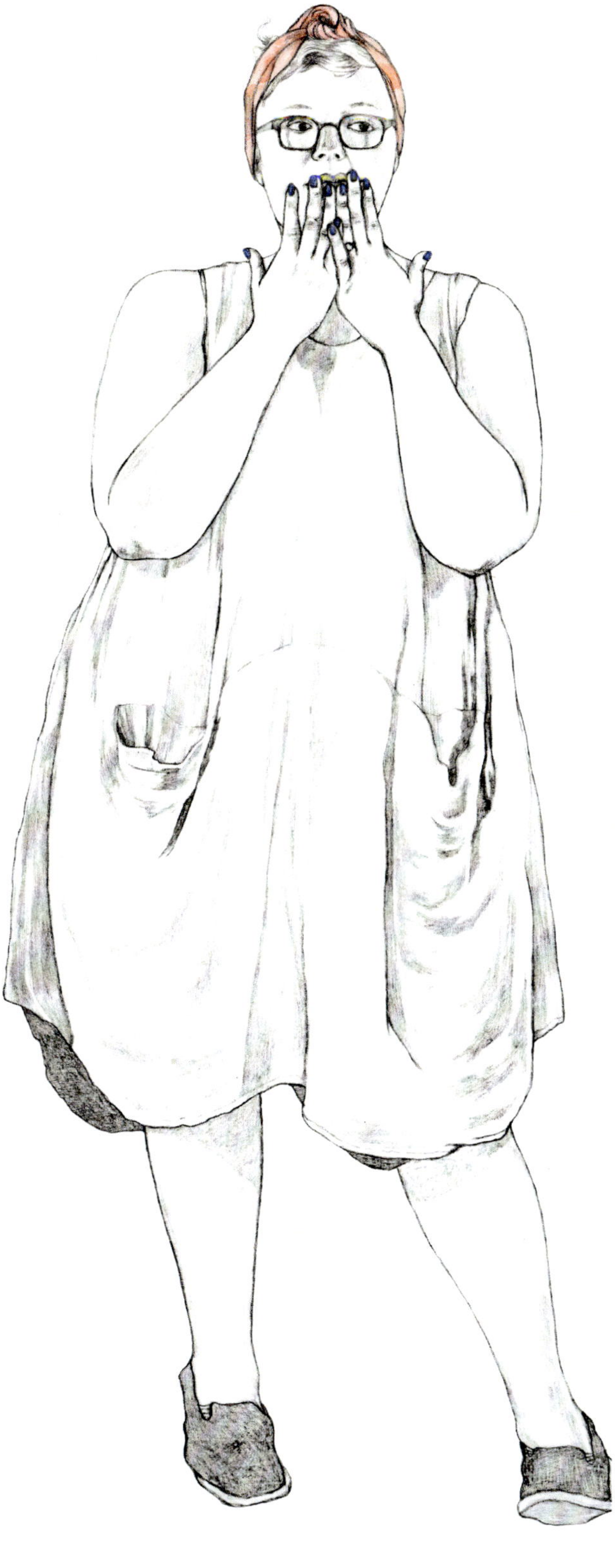

Fig. 35

# Romantic Love

*as portrayed by Julie Atlas Muz and Mat Fraser*

> "*...the most essential of the propensities of love is... the propensity of reunion and community, which, during the most perfect harmony of souls often acquires such a degree of force that if, according to the expression of the comic Greek [Aristophanes], Vulcan should descend from the heavens to unite the two lovers as he would join two pieces of iron by the stroke of his anvil at his forge, he would find them already at the height of their wishes ... Lovers, in grasping hands, or in embracing, yield to this soft propensity; it is this penchant which attracts them. Whilst embracing each other, they unite their glowing cheeks and ardent lips and mutually passing the arms around the neck, alternately repose on the bosom of each other.*"
>
> —Siddons, Letter XIX

The romance is in the squeeze. Lovers embrace. The hand gripping the waist, the middles of the bodies coming together. The bodies hollow to unfold each other. The toes are pointed in, they almost touch, tap toe to toe. The hand clasp, interlacing of fingers. The romance is in the closed eye, a blind gesture. The mouths are romantic, not kissing but smiling.

Romantic Love is double, the coming together creates the romance. An actor will have a hard time delineating Romantic Love if she is repulsed by her partner—this need not be said. What should the actor who is repulsed do? Fall in love for a moment, erase all history, and all future. In the moment, be only bodies coming together. The lover doesn't need this lesson, but how often is a pair of true lovers on the stage?

There can be no guidelines for the clothing of true love, it could be anything, is probably something very simple.

Romantic Love, the squeeze, is: "I want you to know." The intention of the actor is to let the other and the world know that in this moment the bodies come together and look only towards each other. Here we have a rare sample of romantic love that is not threatened by Obstacle, a bird of prey that could be viewing the couple from above, circling towards. Romantic Love is the most and the least dramatic of gestures.

# Acknowledgements

This project began some time in the early twenty-first century with Normandy's first encounter with Henry Siddons' book *Practical Illustrations of Rhetorical Gesture and Action*. Thanks is due to Craig Flanagin, who introduced Normandy to the book, and to Craig's parents, Jon and Judy, who later checked the book out of the University of South Dakota library and mailed it to New York for Normandy to peruse again.

Work on this project began in earnest in 2013 when the NTUSA's Matt Kalman graciously hosted the company for a summer retreat at his house in upstate New York. There we took some of the first photographs for the book, which would ultimately prove unusable. But strides were made in the design of the project. And we returned to the city with a stronger idea of where we wanted to take it. Additional development took place the following summer through an LMCC Process Space Residency on Governor's Island in New York City. The company was workshopping several ideas on the Island that hot summer, and it was there that we took some of the first photographs that would be included in the project. But while many people posed for us, only a few of the images were usable. Thanks is due to Emily Davis, Ryan Holsopple, Juliana Francis-Kelly, David Patrick Kelly, Pete Simpson and Edgar Oliver for being our early test subjects.

Over the course of the next year, Jesse finished the first set of eleven illustrations, based mostly on new photographs, and Normandy wrote commentary to accompany them. This first set of images and text was, in part, made possible by a commission from Ilan Bachrach's Mass Live Arts Festival in Great Barrington, Massachusetts, which hosted a gallery show of the work as part of their 2015 season. And throughout that summer Jesse was hard at work photographing actors for the rest of the project in studio space donated by Celeste Coughlin and in Jesse's own studio in Red Hook. Several props featured in these illustrations, including the ladder, the Vespa scooter and the rocket trophy, were also lent to us by Celeste.

Over the course of the production, there were several actors who posed for us, but whose images we were unable to include in the final production, and still many others with whom we discussed the project and hoped to capture but, due to the restrictions of time and resources (and our own photographic ineptitude), were unable to include here. Special thanks is due to Jason Craig, Jessica Jelliffe and Matt Korahais whom we photographed on the fly, but not well enough. If there is a volume two, it will start with you.

In 2015, Jay Wegman invited us to present the premiere gallery show of the full set of illustrations and text at Abrons Arts Center in New York City, and on several occasions provided studio space to photograph performers. Maedhbh McCullagh became an invaluable liaison between ourselves and Abrons Director of Visual Arts Jonathan Durham as we planned the show for the 2017 season. Thanks is also due to Interim Director of Visual Arts Joshua Lubin-Levy, incoming Visual Arts Coordinator Christopher Watkins, and Abrons new Artistic Director Craig T. Peterson for their support for this project.

Jesse completed a significant portion of the illustrations for this book as a MacDowell Colony fellow in the spring of 2016. And Normandy completed much of her writing for the book while in residence at Yaddo in the winter of 2017. Thanks is due to these invaluable institutions for their support.

Digitization of the original images was made possible by a number of conspirators. The inimitable Maggie Hoffman cleaned up our first set of images and designed the text panels for our 2015 show at Mass Live Arts. Hoffman also mentored us in Photoshop as we took the digital reigns of the project in 2016. Scanning of the original artwork was made possible by Will Saltonstall of Saltonstall Architects and the kind folks of the Imaging Services Office at Harvard's Widener Library. Final scans of the hand colored prints were made by Jaya Miceli at Penguin Books.

Bertie Ferdman read initial drafts of James' introductory essay, offering critical insight and guidance. And Craig Flanagin was a constant reader of Normandy's commentary.

Funding for this project was provided by the Andrew W. Mellon Foundation, the New York Foundation for the Arts, the New York State Council on the Arts and the New York City Department of Cultural Affairs. But the lion's share of support came from individual contributors. Immense gratitude is due to: Roger Aldridge, Judy Bauerlein, Kim Buck, Jonathan Butterick, Janet Clancy, Celeste Coughlin, Marc Dale, Mark Doskow, Bertie Ferdman, Christian Fletcher, Vallejo Gantner, Kate Hawley, Claire Hawley, Molly and Rick Hawley, Sarah Hughes, Matt Kalman, Ali Kenner Brodsky, Trina Basu Ramamurthy, Zoe Rosenfeld, Kate Scelsa, Freddie Scelsa, Scott Shepherd, Vivian Stanley and Jerry Olson, Jeff Stark, Lucy Taylor, Jacob Watson, Lea Watson, Philippa Wehle, Ben Williams, Gary Wilmes, Kristin Worrall and Tally.

And, finally, thanks is due to Karinne Keithley Syers and Antje Oegel of 53rd State Press who along with their team—designer Chris Giarmo and copy editor Jess Barbagallo—supported our belief that this book could be at once a document of our community, an artifact of our time and an object of lasting beauty, and for helping us get it into the world.

# Biographies

## AUTHORS

JESSE HAWLEY (Illustrator, Designer) is an interdisciplinary artist and co-founder of the National Theater of the United States of America, with whom she shares her skills as designer, director, songwriter, choreographer and performer. Since its founding in 2000, she has co-created all of the company's productions, and performed them across NYC, the U.S. and in Dublin, Ireland. Favorite venues include The Public Theater, The Kitchen, PS122, The Chocolate Factory, The Walker Art Center, Mass MoCA, The Stonington Opera House, the basement of an abandoned shoe store in Times Square and the ruins of a former Viking museum in Dublin. Jesse has also worked with notable theater artists Richard Foreman, Juliana Francis Kelly, Ken Nintzel, Mallory Catlett, Yehuda Duenyas, Normandy Sherwood, Young Jean Lee and Erik Ehn, and was a guest artist at the Juilliard school, and had a brief cameo on television in a Conan O'Brien skit entitled *Harry Potter, the Porno*. She illustrated the book *ANIMALS vs. FURNITURE*, written by Normandy Sherwood and published by Ugly Duckling Presse. In 2016 Jesse was a MacDowell Colony fellow, preparing the illustrations for this, the NTUSA's final project, and relocated from NYC to coastal Massachusetts, where she teaches theater at The Tabor Academy, and continues to make new work with partner and collaborator James Stanley.

NORMANDY RAVEN SHERWOOD (Commentary) is theater maker: playwright, costumer, director, performer. Her plays have been presented at many theaters, including The Brick, The New Ohio Theater, The Kitchen, Dixon Place and Skidmore College. She is a member of the OBIE-award-winning National Theater of the United States of America (NTUSA). With the NTUSA has created many spectacular shows including *Chautauqua!, The Golden Veil, Abacus Black!* and *What's That On my Head!?!*—these shows have toured the finest theaters of the United States and the finest basements of New York City. Normandy also makes work with her band/theater company The Drunkard's Wife which has produced shows such as *Permanent Caterpillar*, *Feather Gatherers* and *Tiny Hornets*. She runs Uncanny Valley, a performance parlor in Williamsburg, Brooklyn with her partner Craig Flanagin. She is a MacDowell Colony Fellow and has been an artist in residence at Yaddo, the Millay Colony, the LMCC and chashama. Her children's book, *ANIMALS vs. FURNITURE* (also illustrated by Jesse Hawley) was published by Ugly Duckling Presse in 2013. As a costumer she has designed productions by Classic Stage Company, Joshua William Gelb, New Georges, Mac Wellman, Young Jean Lee, Tina Satter, and Faye Driscoll (Bessie Award, 2009). She is one of the curators of Little Theatre @Dixon Place and she teaches in the Expository Writing Program at NYU. She has an MFA in playwriting from Brooklyn College.

JAMES P. STANLEY (Essay, Editor) is a media scholar and theater artist whose work in both fields mines the history of American spectacle and is a founder and co-artistic director of The National Theater of the United States of America. He authored the company's first two productions, *Garvey & Superpant$* and *Placebo Sunrise*, and has collaborated as a writer, director, designer and performer on all of their work since. As an actor, James has performed in works by Young Jean Lee, Richard Maxwell, Thomas Bradshaw, Hal Hartley, Julie Atlas Muz, Phil Soltanoff, Joanna Settle, Darko Tresnjak and many others. In 2014 James originated the role of Matt in Young Jean Lee's *Straight White Men*, performing in its America and European premieres. The following year, James received his PhD in Media, Culture, and Communication from NYU. He currently works as a Lecturer on History and Literature and on Theater, Dance and Media at Harvard University and continues to make theater and music on the South Coast of Massachusetts with partner and longtime collaborator Jesse Hawley.

THE NATIONAL THEATER OF THE UNITED STATES OF AMERICA (NTUSA) was founded in the bowels of Times Square in 2000 by Ryan Bronz, Mark Doskow, Yehuda Duenyas, Jesse Hawley, Jonathan Jacobs and James Stanley. They were joined shortly thereafter by Normandy Sherwood. Sound Designer Jody Elff and Lighting Designer Ben Kato have contributed to every show. The company members who regularly fueled their work include Ilan Bachrach, Matt Kalman, Aimee McCormick, George Nobl and Ean Sheehy. For their inaugural production *Garvey and Superpant$: Episode #23* a lavish, miniature 1930's era vaudeville theater was constructed in the basement of a dilapidated deli in Times Square. The piece was a popular and critical success, and firmly established the company on the New York theater scene. Since then they have produced 7 other full scale productions, a record of music and this book. Their work has toured nationally and internationally, and has been recognized by multiple awards including an OBIE Award for Design in 2006, a Spalding Gray Award in 2007, the LMCC Presidents Award in 2010 and two Henry Hewes Design Award nominations in 2012. Over the years, NTUSA productions have appeared on several "Best Of..." lists, including Time Out New York (2002), The Village Voice (2006), Brooklyn's L Magazine and the New Yorker (2009). The company's artistic excellence has been recognized with grants from The Greenwall Foundation, The Mellon Foundation, The New York State Council on the Arts, The New York City Department of Cultural Affairs, The Lower Manhattan Cultural Council, and Arts International's DNA project grant, as well as multiple space grants and residencies from chashama, the Chocolate Factory, Two Trees Realty and others.

## ACTORS

Ilan Bachrach is a performer and visual artist raised in Boston and based in Great Barrington, Massachusetts and Brooklyn, New York. He is a company member of Nature Theater of Oklahoma and The National Theater of the United States of America, and has also created and performed in works with Jim Findlay, Phil Soltanoff, Sibyl Kempson, Temporary Distortion, Collapsable Giraffe, Witness Relocation and others.

Jess Barbagallo makes theater with a special interest in the alternating poetry and prose of labor's effects on emotional life. Jess moved to New York City in 2001 to study acting at the Experimental Theatre Wing at New York University. Highlights include meeting the majority of his best friends, pulling a fish from his boxer briefs in a self-scripting class and falling in love with several charismatic actresses. Upon graduating in 2005, Jess began working with Big Dance Theater; his aesthetic has been hugely influenced by the work of BDT founders Annie-B Parson and Paul Lazar, particularly their attention to stage composition and pedestrian abstraction. After waiting tables for a year while rehearsing part-time at the now defunct Stable in Dumbo, Jess decided that turning the entirety of his paycheck over to Sallie Mae every month was enough of a reason to enlist in grad school, to maybe become a teacher and work in the more dignified medium of playwriting. It was there at Brooklyn College, under the tutelage of Mac Wellman, that Jess met Tina Satter. One thing led to ranother and soon Tina and Jess founded a company called Half Straddle together in 2008; they continue to make work and regularly fight about art. Over the years, Jess has acted in pretty much every small theater below 14th Street and toured domestically and internationally with different folks. Favorite projects: creating *Room for Cream: A Live Lesbian Soap Opera* with a cohort of amazing dykes, performing challenging and durational works with Andrea Geyer on film and at museums like the Whitney and the Stedelijk, managing ahead-of-the curve alt-comic Karen Davis for many years and meeting a dog named Bluet in 2011, who continues to support Jess the way only a ten pound animal utterly devoid of human bullshit can.

Kate Benson is a writer and actor living in Brooklyn. Her plays include *A Beautiful Day in November on the Banks of the Greatest of the Great Lakes* (Obie winner), produced by New Georges with the Women's Project Theater in 2015, *[PORTO]*, *Lee Miller*, *Super Magic Wild Forest*, *Radium Now* (produced at Brooklyn College in 2016) and the Assembly's *I Will Look Forward to This Later* (co-writer, with Emily Perkins-Margolin, produced at the New Ohio in 2016). She is a member of the Usual Suspects at NYTW and was in the 2014-15 Soho Rep Writer/Director Lab, and she is a graduate of the Brooklyn College MFA Playwriting program. She is the recipient of the Clubbed Thumb Biennial Commission. Performances include: *I'll Never Love Again* (Bushwick Starr), *Tiger, Tiger (on the Nature of Violence)* (Dixon Place), *Fondly, Collette Richland* (Elevator Repair Service at New York Theater Workshop), *Running Away from the One with the Knife* (the Chocolate Factory), *Nomads* (the Incubator), *Good Person of Szechwan* (the Public and LaMama), *home/sick* (the Assembly at the Living Theater), and *Purity* (PS122). She is a founding member of the performance collective Wook Taut Majesty.

Black-Eyed Susan is a legendary performer in New York experimental theater. A founding member Charles Ludlam's Ridiculous Theatrical Company with whom she collaborated for twenty years, she has also performed with Mabou Mines, Ethyl Eichelberger, John Jesurun, Jim Neu, Taylor Mac and many others. In 1986 she received an Obie award for Sustained Excellence of Performance, and in 2014 received a Foundation for Contemporary Arts Grants to Artists award.

Nikki Calonge is a performer and theater maker. Born in the Philippines and raised in Virginia, she received her BFA from New York University/Tisch School of the Arts' Experimental Theatre Wing and Playwrights Horizons Theater School, trained in The Patravadi Theatre with Theater Mitu in Thailand, and studied Traditional Dance and Wayang Kulit in Bali, Indonesia. Since graduating, Nikki has had the great pleasure of performing with artists and theater companies such as Nellie Tinder, Hoi Polloi, Half Straddle, Katherine Brook/TELE-VIOLET, Eliza Bent + Dave Malloy, Spellbound Theater, William Burke, Normandy Raven Sherwood/Drunkard's Wife and The National Asian American Theater Company. In 2011 she became a founding member of ANIMALS performance group and a member of Witness Relocation. With ANIMALS she is the recipient of the 2012 Tom Murrin Award, part of *Paper Magazine*'s 2012 Beautiful People Issue, and has been presented at Fresh Ground Pepper, CATCH, Prelude, as part of Target Margin Theater's Gertrude Stein Lab and Under the Radar's Incoming Series. Aside from live performance, Nikki participates in film projects, most notably Andrea Geyer's Comrades of Time, Eva von Schweinitz's Heads or Tails and Dr. Anton Juan's Hinabing Pakpak ng Ating mga Anak. Nikki's own work is highly collaborative, physically rigorous and spiritually charged. She maintains a regular practice in Yoga and Aikido to support the creative process.

Maxwell Cosmo Cramer is a performer based in New York City. He grew up in Redding, CT with his parents Ellen and David and siblings Milo and Phoebe. <3. As a child, Max played a character named Turkey Man who was always naked. One time, dressed as a devil, he stabbed his father's eye with a toy pitchfork. Also, he frequently prepped but never performed a recreation of the burning tower scene from Dumbo. He has studied acting at Bard College, BADA, HB Studios, UCB, One on One, Bread and Puppet, independently in Berlin, and beyond. Since 2009, he has worked with theater artists Normandy Sherwood, John Jahnke, 600 Highwaymen, Michael Laub, New Saloon, Ariel Stess, Claire Moodey, Milo Cramer, Phoebe Cramer, Morgan Green, Johanna McKeon and Meghan Finn, among others; performance artist Allison Brainard; filmmakers Annelise Ogaard, Margarita Jimeno, Orit Ben-Shitrit and Zbigniew Bzymek. He also writes copy, works at restaurants, draws little faces and likes clothes.

Faye Driscoll is a Bessie Award-winning choreographer and director whose work is rooted in an obsession with the problem of being "somebody" in a world of other "somebodies." Originally from Venice Beach, California, Driscoll moved to New York in 1994 to train in dance at Tisch School of the Arts at NYU. She began her career dancing with groups such as Yasmeen Godder, David Neumann and Doug Varone and Dancers. In 2005 she started making her own work, aiming to create immersive worlds of sensorial complexity and perceptual disorientation, one where awkward virtuosic bodies teeter on the edge of high art and slapstick. These investigations gave rise to a wide range of works including: *Loneliness* (2006), exhibited in the Younger Than Jesus triennial at the New Museum; *Wow, Wow, Wow* (2007), a postmodern/pop musical/death metal fantasy; *837 Venice Boulevard* (2008, Bessie Award), an autobiographical work within a theater within a home; *There Is So Much Mad In Me* (2010), an exploration of ecstatic states; *You're Me* (2012), a duet distorted by props, paint and manic costume shifts; and *Thank You For Coming: Attendance* (2014), and *Thank You For Coming: Play* (2016), the first and second parts respectively in a series of works that propose performance as a shared political act, where performer and audience co-create reality. Her work has been presented across the country at places such as Walker Art Center, Wexner Center for the Arts, ICA/Boston, Danspace Project and American Dance Festival, and internationally in Argentina, France and Croatia.

Aleta Findlay is a middle school student in Brooklyn, NY. She has appeared as Frances Griffiths in Tony Oursler's 5D film *Imponderable*, which was shown at the Museum of Modern Art, and Jim Findlay's productions *Vine of the Dead* (Invisible Dog, 2016; Collapsable Hole Westbeth, 2015) and *Dream of a Red Chamber* (Brill Building, 2013). Other favorite roles have included Mary Lennox in *The Secret Garden* (2016) and Patty Simcox in *Grease* (2015). Aleta is an avid climber and a member of BKBeasts at Brooklyn Boulders. She also enjoys singing and playing piano and is a founding member of the band Community Council.

Jim Findlay works across boundaries as a theater artist, visual artist and filmmaker. His most recent work includes his original performances *Vine of the Dead* (2015), *Dream of the Red Chamber* (2014) and the direction and design of David Lang's *Whisper Opera* as well as the unreleased 3D film *Botanica*. His video installation in collaboration with Ralph Lemon, *Meditation*, is in the permanent collection of the Walker Art Center. He was a founding member of the Collapsable Giraffe and in partnership with Radiohole founded the Collapsable Hole, a multi-disciplinary artist led performance venue recently relocated to Manhattan's West Village. In addition to his work as an independent artist, he maintains a long career as a collaborator with many theater, performance and music artists including Mallory Catlett, Daniel Fish, Aaron Landsman, The Wooster Group, Ridge Theater, Bang on a Can, Ralph Lemon, and Stew and Heidi Rodewald. His work has been seen at Lincoln Center, Carnegie Hall, BAM, Arena Stage, A.R.T. and over 50 cities internationally. In 2015 he received the Foundation for Contemporary Art Grants to Artists award, and his previous awards include three Obies, two Bessies, two Princess Grace Awards, Lucille Lortel and Henry Hewes Design Awards and residencies at Baryshnikov Arts Center, the MacDowell Colony, UCross, MassMOCA and Mount Tremper Arts.

After graduating from Duke University with a degree in Chinese History, Ari Fliakos returned to his native NY, where he took the logical next step of performing and creating work with and for award-winning theater ensemble The Wooster Group. Over the past twenty years he has developed and originated performances in *House/Lights*, *To You*, *The Birdie!*, *Poor Theater* (for which he won an Obie Award), *Who's Your Dada?!*, *La Didone*, *Hamlet* (as Claudius, Public Theater), *Vieux Carré*, *Early Plays* (directed by Richard Maxwell), *Cry Trojans!* (in collaboration with the Royal Shakespeare Company), *Harold Pinter's The Room* and *The Town Hall Affair*. As a core company member, he also appeared in *Brace Up! (Three Sisters)*, *Fish Story*, *Hairy Ape* and *North Atlantic*. He has toured internationally and throughout the US and internationally to Santiago, Bogota, São Paolo, London, Paris, Dijon, Hong Kong, Barcelona, Athens and Warsaw. Ari has been narrating audiobooks since 2011. Recent titles include *The Nix* by Nathan Hill and *Here I Am*, by Jonathan Safran Foer. His narration for Seth Patrick's *Reviver* received an Audie Award in 2013. He and Erin Douglass run their own Brooklyn renovation and real estate business, housebywe, out of their home and office of 11 years in Bedford Stuyvesant, Brooklyn.

Juliana Francis-Kelly has originated roles for many great writer/directors in the U.S, Asia and Europe, including Reza Abdoh (as a founding member of the internationally acclaimed Dar A Luz Company); Richard Foreman (in *Paradise*

*Hotel*; *Bad Boy Nietzsche!*; *King Cowboy Rufus Rules the Universe* and *Maria Del Bosco*—for which she received an Obie Award) and for Anne Bogart, Young Jean Lee, Pavol Liska and Kelly Copper, Lear deBessonet, Normandy Sherwood, Hal Hartley, Meredith Drum, Mary Billyou, Marie Losier in collaboration with Guy Maddin, Karin Conrad (at BAM and The Folger Shakespeare Library); and David Michalek (for Lincoln Center Festival's Portraits in Dramatic Time). Ms. Kelly also makes her own work. Plays include: *The Reenactors*, directed by Tony Torn at Abrons Arts Center; *Go Go Go*, directed by Anne Bogart for PS122, and reprised at The Institute of Contemporary Art for London International Festival of Theater; *Box*, directed by Torn and performed at The Women's Project, PS122 and The Fontanon Festival in Italy; and *The Baddest Natashas*, directed by Torn and performed at The Ontological Theater. Her plays have been translated into Italian, Greek, German and Norwegian, and published in the U.S. and Europe. Ms. Kelly also writes for film companies and builds mix-media dolls. She lives in NYC with her husband, actor-musician David Patrick Kelly and their daughter, who also does plays sometimes.

Mat Fraser is a multi-disciplinary performing artist, actor, writer and musician, who over the last 18 years has played to audiences from the Olympic Stadium in London and the Royal Albert Hall to many dive bars and late night clubs in NYC and elsewhere, all the while working as a Disability Artist within mainstream arts environments. Recently he starred as "Paul the Illustrated Seal" in FX's *American Horror Story: Freak Show*, and in 2013 he and his partner in art and life Julie Atlas Muz, created an adult, hit version of *Beauty and the Beast* through their company ONEOFUS. His recent museum site specific solo show *Cabinet of Curiosities: How Disability Was Kept in a Box*, won the UK's Observer Ethical Award for Arts & Entertainment in 2014, and he's just finished writing a new stage play, *A Multitude of Elvii*. Fraser was a drummer with a number of rock bands including Fear of Sex, Living in Texas and, currently, The Spazms.

David Greenspan is an actor and playwright perhaps best known for acting in his plays *Dead Mother*, *She Stoops to Comedy*, *Go Back to Where You Are* and *I'm Looking for Helen Twelvetrees*. He is also recognized for his solo renditions of Barry Conners' 1925 comedy *The Patsy*; Gertrude Stein's lecture "Plays" and a program of Stein lectures and a playlet *Composition...Masterpieces...Identity*; and his solo plays *The Myopia* and *The Argument*. Additional acting credits include premieres by David Adjmi, Sarah Ruhl, Adam Rapp, Stephin Merritt, William Hoffman, Terrence McNally, David Grimm, Kathleen Tolan, Richard Foreman, Mac Wellman, Jeffrey M. Jones, and his association with the work of director David Herskovits at Target Margin Theater. He enjoys close collaborative relationships with directors Leigh Silverman and Jack Cummings III, and is the recipient of Guggenheim and Fox fellowships, Alpert and Lambda Literary awards and five Obies.

Jenn Harris has performed off-Broadway in *SILENCE! THE MUSICAL*, *Modern Orthodox* (Lucille Lortel Award and Theatre World Award), *All In The Timing*, *The Understudy*, *New Jerusalem*, *Mercy on the Doorstep*, BTF's *Pageant Play* and *The Heidi Chronicles*. In regional theater she has performed at The Old Globe in The Women and In Your Arms; at The Wilma in The Understudy; at the Williamstown Theater Festival in *Blithe Spirit*, *God of Vengeance*, *The Winter's Tale* and *Street Scene*; and at the The Muny in *Hairspray*. In New York City she performed in *The Plank Project* and has made many appearances at the long running downtown pop revue showcase *My Hit Parade* at Joe's Pub. Jenn's solo show *The Moment You've Been Waiting Four* opened at the Duplex in 2015. She has appeared in the films *Gayby* (Official Selection SXSW 2012), *5 Doctors*, *Better Living Through Chemistry*, *Fits and Starts*, *A Case of You*, *Confessions of a Shopaholic*; and has appeared on television in *Difficult People*, *High Maintenance*, *30 Rock*, *Eastsiders*, *Alpha House*, *Mother's Day*, *Bored to Death*, *Law & Order* and *L&O CSI*. Jenn studied at Boston University's School for the Arts, LAMDA and Second City in Chicago. In 2016, Jenn co-wrote, produced and starred in the web series *New York Is Dead*. She makes Barbie art and music videos for her website Bucketofcuddles.com.

Ryan Holsopple is a designer, performer and programmer. His wide ranging body of work includes sound design for Jim Findlay's *Vine of the Dead* at Westbeth Arts and Radiohole's *Tarzana* at The Performing Garage; video for Annie Dorsen's *Yesterday Tomorrow* at the Holland Festival; interaction design for Mallory Catlett's *This Was The End* at The Chocolate Factory; associate video design for Annie Dorsen's *A Piece of Work* at BAM's Next Wave 2013 and Seattle's On The Boards festival; interaction design for Radiohole's *Inflatable Frankenstein* at The Kitchen; interaction design for Mantra Percussion's performance of *Timber* by Michael Gordon at BAM; programming laser pointer audience interaction for Bill Morrison's *Shooting Gallery* at BAM's Next Wave 2012 ; and plant interaction design for Jim Findlay's *Botanica* at 3LD. Ryan is the founder of the performance group 31 Down and has performed and designed sound for all of 31 Down's performances including: *dataPurge* (PS122), *Here At Home* (Bushwick Starr), *Red Over Red* (Incubator Arts Project), *The Assembler Dilator* (PS122), and *That's Not How Mahler Died* (Ontological Theater). Ryan received a Doris Duke Charitable Trust Grant with PS122 to develop a new technological performance program for PS122, and won a Bessie Award for design for Mallory Catlett's *This Was The End* in 2014. He was nominated for the 2011 Henry Hewes Design Award for sound design of 31 Down's *Here At Home*. And 31 Down was listed as a Best of New York 2007 by the Village Voice for their interactive telephone murder mystery set in the New York Subway system called *Canal Street Station*, co-produced by free103point9 Transmission Arts. Ryan is a graduate of NYU's Interactive Telecommunications Program and currently teaches Dynamic and Interactive Media Performance in the PIMA Graduate Program at Brooklyn College. Ryan has also taught radio communication at the College of Staten Island.

Mike Iveson is a performer and composer based in New York City. He works most often with Elevator Repair Service theater company, appearing in *Gatz*, *The Sound and the Fury*, and as narrator Jake Barnes in the company's adaptation of an Ernest Hemingway novel, *The Select (The Sun Also Rises)*, among others. He has performed extensively with choreographer Sarah Michelson and legendary performance art duo DANCENOISE as well as many other theater artists. He has toured as a pianist with the New York City Players and in Sibyl Kempson's *Crime or Emergency*. His own plays with music, *Sorry Robot* and *The Tear Drinkers*, have been produced in New York to a certain acclaim. He teaches theater to public school teens every summer in The Wooster Group Summer Institute.

Mikéah Ernest Jennings is an art theater and performance creator from the Mojave Desert. Interested mainly in the inutility of the 4th wall, Mikéah pursues collaborations with artists who reframe the conventional audience/performer relationship as way to highlight the performance of the audience as an equally vital component of the theatrical ritual. At an early age Mikéah was interested in a career as an illustrator and animator, but an early involvement with dance led to an introduction to theater and acting, and Mikéah has focused on performance ever since. Mikéah has collaborated with a number of artists currently shaping the face of contemporary performance, including Charlotte Brathwaite, Lila Neugebauer (*The Signature Plays*), Young Jean Lee (*The Shipment*), Dan Rothenberg/Pig Iron Theatre (*I Promised Myself to Live Faster*), Caden Manson/Big Art Group and Jay Scheib (*World of Wires*). In 2013 Mikéah made his first foray into academia accepting an adjunct faculty position in the Department of Music and Theater at Massachusetts Institute of Technology, and, in 2016, designed the course "Live Media in Performance: an introduction to live-feed-camera performance on stage" for the Department of Theater at the New School for Social Research.

Ayesha Jordan is a multi-disciplinary performance artist who often uses characters and stories to create indelible moments in experiences that are both cerebral and visceral. Jordan's characters each represent a facet of herself and act as a tool to playfully disguise herself, and to uniquely connect with guests. Her work aims to create a feeling of authenticity and genuineness that relates directly to who she is as a person. Much of Jordan's work is about audience engagement, bringing participants as close to the work as possible–creating moments, tasks and prompts that allow the opportunity to engage with the performer, as well as with fellow audience members. Some of her previous performance events include *Shasta Geaux Pop* (Under The Radar Festival and The Bushwick Starr), *Come See My Double D's* (JACK), *Enter & Exit: Playing House* (JACK), *Enter & Exit: Family Reunion* (JACK), *Inter 1-to-1* and *In the Tube*. Other works include the video projects *Living Room Dance Breaks*, *Drunk & Famous* and a host of other songs and videos. Jordan has also been seen as an actor in the Broadway production of *Eclipsed* by Danai Gurira and directed by Liesl Tommy; *Ludic Proxy* by Aya Ogawa (The Play Company); *Platonov: Or the Disinherited* by Jay Scheib (The Kitchen); and *Harold I Hate You* by Cakeface (Ars Nova & Triskelion), as well as in video work and photography by visual artist Carrie Mae Weems.

Matt Kalman is an actor, writer and filmmaker currently living in Brooklyn, NY. In 1994, Matt moved to New York City to pursue a career in acting. While making the rounds, wasting time, waiting on long lines, and attending countless cattle call auditions, Matt appeared in dozens of plays, musicals and films, most of which left him feeling frustrated and empty. He then decided to take matters into his own hands and began writing plays that challenged the norms and forms of conventional theater while remaining accessible and entertaining to a more general public. In 2003 he adapted one such play into a feature film which played in festivals around the country. Since then, Matt has made his living in film as a writer, editor, producer and director. However, Matt never completely abandoned the live arts. For the past fifteen years, he has found similar sensibilities in the National Theater of the United States of America (NTUSA), developing, performing and documenting almost all of their works and touring around the globe. Currently Matt divides his time between raising a family, homesteading in upstate New York, making money in the city and exercising his artistic muscles in whichever way presents itself.

David Patrick Kelly ... the choreography of emotion ... the significant gesture evolves for me from ... the highest poetics ... which can be found in the lowest of genres ... always aspired to Theatre of Poetry ... word becoming flesh ... Shakespeare, Euripides, Chekhov, Büchner, Foreman, Gogol, Hammett, Studs Terkel, Zola, Gombrowicz, Albee, Shepard ... trained always toward physical theatre inspired probably by Grotowski and rock and roll ... studied Mime in Paris with Marcel Marceau ... saw Ariane Mnouchkine, LaMama and Cat Stevens ... came to New York first to study at Merce Cunningham ... then Ballet, Kunju Opera, Shaolin Kung Fu, Seido Karate, Yoga ... an eccentric personal Stanislavski training from the great Mira Rostova ... inspiration from seeing Beatles (their famous formal bow suggested by their RADA trained manager) ... Hendrix, Doors, MC5, Springsteen, Wailers, Suicide, Iggy and the Psychedelic Stooges, James Chance, Television, Patti Smith, Lydia Lunch, New York Dolls ... Artaud (a great movie actor) ... had a List of What Theatre Should Be (my career guide) and I checked off many items ... busking as training ground ... street performers ... the immediacy

Sibyl Kempson is the founder of the 7 Daughters of Eve Thtr. & Perf. Co. in New York City. She writes and directs—and sometimes still performs in—plays, rituals, ceremonies and installations with this company and its many wonderful members. She values solitude and learning, but also enjoys collaborating with others very much, and sharing ideas, and is very lucky to have contributed to the work of other artists in New York since 1996, at many splendid and memorable venues throughout the United States and the World. Sibyl spends a lot of time working on her relationship with Nature, and deepening her awareness and skills so as to be better able to communicate the meaning of that relationship to other humans. When she was a little child, she believed that everything was alive and had feelings. And now that belief seems to be coming true. She is discovering that the languages of nature and human spirituality are closely linked, and consists of images and symbols imparted to us and from us, in visions and dreams from a vast shared consciousness. Her work is becoming very much about re-connecting the modern mind with those ancient tools of perception and understanding, whilst also having a real good time. To that end, she is currently making a series of performance rituals for the Whitney Museum of American Art called *12 Shouts to the Ten Forgotten Heavens*, taking place on all solstices and equinoxes through 2018. Intersecting with that project will be *Sasquatch Rituals*, which will also be performed at Abrons Arts Center and deep in the woods late at night. Connected to that project will be *The Securely Conferred, Vouchsafed Keepsakes of Maery S.*, a play with songs, which will follow in 2018. Sibyl studied playwriting at Brooklyn College.

Aaron Landsman makes performances using people, language, space and time. He often starts with questions: how does technology affect the ways we remember? How do we perform power, and who gets to play which roles? Can the person who made you who you are be the person who messed you up, be the person you forgive now? Some of his work is co-authored with community members over long periods of time; some is developed through ongoing relationships with other artists; all of it honors collaboration as a driving force. Some constant collaborators include Mallory Catlett, Jim Findlay, Brent Green, Paul Shambroom, Henry Street Settlement and GOLES. He writes about misfits, overheard spaces and people, the ways we welcome each other or don't. The forms he has explored include: a project with urban planners and young people on the Lower East Side; a play in a theater about suicide and religious faith; a nighttime country busride that includes a story about landscape and memory, projected video and original music; a participatory performance in five cities, combining transcripts of local government meetings, original writing and video, and deep local collaboration; a performance drawn from 583 anonymous cast-off photos at a single lab in the 1970s.

Paul Lazar is a founding member and co-artistic director, along with Annie-B Parson, of Big Dance Theater. He has co-directed and acted in works for Big Dance since 1991, including commissions from the Brooklyn Academy of Music, the Walker Art Center, Dance Theater Workshop, Classic Stage Company and Japan Society. Outside of Big Dance, Paul directed Christina Masciotti's *Social Security* at the Bushwick Starr in 2015, *Elephant Room* at St. Ann's Warehouse for the company Rainpan 43 in 2012, and Young Jean Lee's Obie Award–winning *We're Gonna Die* in 2011. He directed a new version of *We're Gonna Die* in 2015, featuring David Byrne, at the Meltdown Festival in London. He also directed *Bodycast: An Artist Lecture* by Suzanne Bocanegra starring Frances McDormand for the 2014 BAM Next Wave Festival; and *Major Bang* for The Foundry Theatre at St. Ann's Warehouse. Paul is an Associate Member of The Wooster Group, acting in *Brace Up!*, *Emperor Jones*, *North Atlantic* and *The Hairy Ape*. Other stage acting credits include *Tamburlaine* at Theatre for a New Audience, Young Jean Lee's *Lear*, *The Three Sisters* at Classic Stage Company, Richard Maxwell's *Cowboys and Indians* at Soho Rep, *Richard III* at Classic Stage Company, *Svejk* at Theatre for a New Audience, Maria Irene Fornes' *Mud* at the Signature Theatre, and Mac Wellman's *1965 UU*. He has acted in over 30 feature films, including *Snowpiercer*, *The Host*, *Mickey Blue Eyes*, *Silence of the Lambs*, *Beloved*, *Lorenzo's Oil* and *Philadelphia*. His awards include two Bessies, in 2010 and 2002, the Jacob's Pillow Creativity Award in 2007, the Prelude Festival's Frankie Award in 2014, and an Obie Award for Big Dance in 2000. Paul teaches regularly at New York University. He has also taught at Yale, Rutgers, The William Esper Studio and The Michael Howard Studio.

Brian Mendes was trained in theater by the Jesuits of Boston College and Thomas McKenna at the Abbey Theatre in Dublin, Ireland. From there he moved to Chicago and, with Richard Maxwell, Kate Gleason and Gary Wilmes, co-founded the Cook County Theatre Department of Chicago. While with CCTD, Brian directed *Nothing* and *Advertising, Minutes and Seconds* and *Tosca*, and acted in *Clowns Plus Wrestlers*, *Elimination*, *Swing Your Lady* and *Fable*. He was also on the television series *The Untouchables*. After a brief hiatus in Los Angeles, he moved to New York to work with Richard Maxwell and NYC Players. With NYC Players he has acted in *Henry IV*, *Joe*, *The End of Reality* (for which he was also a fight choreographer), *Ode to the Man Who Kneels*, *The Frame*, *The Darkness of this Reading*, *Das Maedchen*, *Open Rehearsal*, *Isolde* and *The Evening*, and directed *People Without History*. He also played Yank in The Wooster Group's production, *Early Plays*. In Berlin he played Helen Steeply in The Hau's production of *Infinite Jest*. He has worked with Adam Rapp (*Animals and Plants* and *Through the Yellow Hour*) and Annie Baker (*The Last of the Little Hours* at Sundance Theatre Lab). As a monologist, he has performed the work of James Tyson and Intangible Studios and was commissioned to present a live video performance of the poetry of Tom King for *Lleisiau/Voices*, a show produced with Chapter in Cardiff,

Wales as part of the hundred year centenary celebrations of Dylan Thomas. He has acted in the plays of Tory Vasquez, Christina Masciotti, and Andrew Ondrejcak, and the films of Redmond Entwistle, Mary Billyou and Danny Dwyer. Most recently he collaborated with saxophonist Bob Feldman on Saxophone, a group telling of the story of a jazz musician growing up in NYC. He has also directed the work of bilingual storyteller and solo performer Antonio Sacre. Brian has performed internationally in many countries including Germany, Sweden, Belgium, Wales, England, Italy, The Netherlands, France, Switzerland, Ireland, Iceland, and most recently with Gekidan Kaitaisha in Tokyo, Japan. Brian is also a songwriter and guitar player with the Brooklyn-based Americana band, The Habit. And he is a kickboxer.

Johanna S. Meyer is a choreographer and performer based in New York City. Comedic and intricate, her work sometimes employs video and often draws on historical material such as burlesque routines, medical textbooks and vintage films, working with highly defined lines of space to execute these ideas. In addition to her own work, Meyer has choreographed for theater works by DJ Mendel, Robert Cucuzza, Ann de Mare, Juliana Francis, Tory Vazquez, Mallory Catlett and Ken Nintzel, among others. She has been a movement consultant for Richard Maxwell in the original version of *Caveman*. Her choreography was featured at the Williamstown Theatre Festival in a production of Chuck Mee's *Big Love* directed by Amanda Charlton. Johanna choreographed by Judy Bauerlein at the University of California at Santa Barbara Summer Theater Lab facilitated by Naomi Iizuka, and choreographed a video project with Marie Losier and Genesis P-orridge. Meyer has also performed in the work of numerous choreographers and directors, including Obie-winner Richard Maxwell, Tory Vazquez, Nami Yamamoto, Karen Sherman and Tanya Gagne, Reggie Wilson/ Fist and Heel, and Nina Martin. She holds a BFA in dance from New York University's Tisch School of the Arts and an MFA in Dance at the University of Illinois at Urbana-Champaign.

Julie Atlas Muz, one of the most acclaimed and prolific conceptual performers and choreographers in New York, sucker punches the boundaries between performance art, dance and burlesque with dark, twisted, come-hither performances that have secured her place in the underworld of nightlife as well as the bastion of the art world. With her signature feminist glamour, Julie tells stories that are beautiful, political and emotional, with a bold and theatrical irreverence all through the power of dance. A Whitney Biennial Artist, a Valencia Biennial Artist, Ethyl Eichelberger Award Recipient, Lambent Fellow, and a Franklin Furnace Artist, Julie has also been deemed "Royalty of Burlesque" by the New York Times, winning both Miss Exotic World and Miss Coney Island 2006. Fraternizing with artists in Ho Chi Minh City, playing Vivien Leigh as Blanche DuBois in North Carolina or touring France while dancing inside a giant balloon, Julie has been named one of *Time Out*'s most fashionable New Yorkers. In a first for contemporary Burlesque artists, Julie has franchised her award winning acts in Las Vegas (*Absinthe* and *Zombie Burlesque*), Dubai (*The Act*), France (*Cabaret New Burlesque*) and Australia (*Absinthe*). In 2016 Julie directed two music videos: *Sunlight* for Amanda Palmer and *Radioactive Japanese Jellyfish* for The Spazms. Her partner in life and love is Mat Fraser with whom she has founded ONEOFUS, an art cell that has created many successful shows including the critically acclaimed *Beauty and the Beast*, *The Freak and the Showgirl* and *ASSFREAKS*.

Okwui Okpokwasili works at the intersection of dance, theater and installation; her concerns in performance are with shaping a shared psychic space untethered from traditional narrative or choreographic structures. She explores the kinetics of empathy. Okpokwasili has received three Bessie Awards for her work in three productions including two original works. Other residencies and awards include the Maggie Allesee National Center for Choreography Choreographic Fellowship (2012, 2016), the Foundation for Contemporary Arts' Artist Grant in Dance (2014), the Rauschenberg Residency (2015), participation in the Lower Manhattan Cultural Council's Extended Life Program 2013-16, as well as the LMCC 2016 Presidential Award for Excellence in the Performing Arts. Okpokwasili is currently the 2015-2017 Randjelovic/Stryker New York Live Arts Resident Commissioned Artist.

Edgar Oliver arrived in New York in 1977 at the age of 21. He began performing in the early 1980's—at the Pyramid nightclub on Avenue A and at ABC No Rio—a gallery on Rivington Street. He wrote and performed poems—and soon these performances became dramatic monologues, with sets painted by his sister—the artist Helen Oliver—now known as Helen Oliver Adelson. One early monologue is based on a long poem called "Prince Lear's Playground." Another early monologue of which he is proud is called "The Poetry Killer." His first play was staged at the Pyramid, and was commissioned by the Pyramid's director, Bobby Bradley. It was called *Motel Blue 19* and was an early incarnation of a play with that same title that later premiered at LaMama. From 1988 to 2001, Edgar premiered a new play or monologue in the club at LaMama almost every year often opening around Halloween—always with sets by his sister Helen. Among these plays and monologues are *The Seven Year Vacation*, *Motel Blue 19*, *Hands in Wartime*, *Mosquito Succulence*, *The Lost Bedroom* and *The Drowning Pages*. Over the years Edgar has performed in works by other downtown playwrights—most notably in plays by Kestutis Nakas, John Epperson (aka Lypsinka), the great drag artist Hapi Phace, and Randall Sharp—the director of the Axis Theatre Company- of which Edgar is a member. Edgar's most notable recent works are three long dramatic monologues: *East 10th Street: Self-portrait with Empty House*—about his years living in an old rooming house on 10th Street (Edinburgh Fringe First Award 2009); *Helen and Edgar*—based on his childhood (2012); and *In the Park*—about his life now and his wanderings in Prospect Park (2014).

Radiohole is an ensemble founded by and comprised of Erin Douglass, Eric Dyer, Maggie Hoffman and Scott Halvorsen Gillette that makes loud, brash and often soggy collaborative shows in the liminal space between theater, performance art, literature, sound and visual art, where conventional rules and categories shift unpredictably. Described by The Drama Review as "the quintessential American performance group," Radiohole's thirteen original productions and numerous short performance works have earned them a reputation as one of NYC's most uncompromising experimental theater companies. After performing in bars and basements around North Brooklyn and the East Village in the late 1990s, Radiohole, (in partnership with The Collapsable Giraffe) founded the original Collapsable Hole in 2000 where most of their work was performed until the venue's closing in 2013. Additionally Radiohole has performed at PS122, The Kitchen, The Performing Garage, LaMama, The Knitting Factory and WFMU's Monty Hall. Nationally their work has toured to Seattle, Minneapolis, Pittsburgh and Troy, NY and internationally, Radiohole has toured to Austria, Denmark, Holland, Ireland and Norway.

Kourtney Rutherford has been involved in theater since she was a child. The youngest of five children, Kourtney's mother was a self-taught visual artist, and her father a train dispatcher. She grew up in Washington State, where she got her start performing small roles in community theater. Exposed to New York performance through late-night cable television, and driven by an obsession with the independent film movement of the early 90s, Kourtney moved to New York in 1994 to study at New York University's Tisch School of the Arts. At NYU, she creatively flourished, training at the Lee Strasberg Institute, the Experimental Theatre Wing, abroad in Russia, Bulgaria and the Netherlands, and taking additional coursework in NYU's film school. A student of Annie-B Parson's choreography class, Kourtney was hired professionally by Annie-B Parson and Paul Lazar's Big Dance Theater in 1997 and continues to work with them. Kourtney co-founded The Operating Theater with Jason Schuler in 2004, and together they have produced numerous works for stage and video. Kourtney's own performance work has appeared throughout New York City, notably at The Kitchen, PS122 and Little Theater. She has worked with some of downtown theater's most cutting edge ensembles including Half Straddle, Witness Relocation and Radiohole, as well as in the plays of Sibyl Kempson, Normandy Sherwood, Eliza Bent and Kenny Finkle. In addition to her work onstage, Kourtney is a theater educator, having earned a master's degree in educational theater in 2012 from City College. She co-founded The Westside Experiment at IRT, an annual summer camp for teens that pairs a working theater artist with students to create an original show. She has been a classroom teacher and teaching artist throughout the New York City public school system, specializing in integrating social studies and English language learning with theater. Kourtney married French musician Mathieu Eveillard in 2013, and has started to act in the French language. A lifelong student, her parallel interests to theater include learning how to write poetry, play guitar and sing duets with her husband.

For Kate Scelsa, twenty years of performing while writing on the side has given way to a life of mostly writing while performing on the side. Kate's first book, *Fans of the Impossible Life*, came out in the fall of 2015. It's about gay teens and for gay teens and also anyone who has feelings. A new book about feminism and social media trolls and reality TV and pop stars and the challenges of self-empowerment will be out soon, also from HarperCollins. A third of the way into that twenty years of performing, Kate became a member of Elevator Repair Service, a company that likes to make shows that play around with text and books. Kate has performed all over the world with ERS, and helped them make a bunch of shows, including the eight hour long Gatz. She writes her own work for theater as well and has a podcast with her dad, legendary New York DJ Vin Scelsa, in which they talk about the history of music and radio in New York. *The Kate and Vin Scelsa Podcast* is distributed on iTunes and SoundCloud. Kate lives in Brooklyn with her wife and their two black cats. This is how you can tell that she is a witch.

Magin Schantz is a community-based artist and performer who builds creative engagement opportunities between disparate groups. Over nearly twenty years in New York she has trained with a variety of theater makers, including Anne

Bogart & the SITI Company, Philippe Gaulier, Steve Wang, Ruth Maleczech, Jonathan Hart, and has collaborated with companies and collectives internationally. She has worked extensively in the visual artists, cultivating skills in painting, printmaking, assemblage, book arts, video art and animation. After a decade of performing and producing theater she returned to school at Pratt Institute to pursue an MS in Art and Design Education, focusing on education as experience and the theatricality of teaching. She uses creativity as a means of making connections, aiming to bridge the gap between the art and experimental theater worlds and those who lack exposure to art or art-making. The need to create, the desire to invent and solve problems aesthetically, the loss of one's self in an idea, is what drives her work. She is currently engaged in several projects: an intergenerational mixed-media art project called Artifact and Fantasy; a performance piece and investigation of terror and nostalgia called Survival Party; a series of videos, untitled, re-enacting humiliating memories from her past; development of an art program with her local CBO in Ridgewood, Queens; and, the rearing of her daughter Mosie (in collaboration with her firefighter husband, Pete). She is grateful to know and work with so many talented and gracious artists in New York, many of whom are featured in this book.

Ean Sheehy graduated from Bard College as a Drama/Dance major before moving to New York in 1994. Within a few years he had met John McCormack, then Artistic Director of the Naked Angels Theater Company, where he became a regular performer, doing readings and workshops of new plays. Here he met the playwright Warren Leight, who had just won a Tony Award for Side Man. The two began working together frequently, on plays such as *Glimmer, Glimmer and Shine* at The Ensemble Studio of Cincinnati and *No Foreigners Beyond This Point* at Center Stage Baltimore. When Mr. Leight began writing for *Law & Order*, he created a character specifically for Ean to play, that of Forensic Accountant Joshua Simmons, drawing on his talent for humor and sympathetic characters. He first became involved with the National Theater of The United States of America in their production of Moliere's *Don Juan*. He found like minds in their collaborative, rule-breaking style and went on to work with them in *Chautauqua!* and *The Golden Veil*, and in Normandy Sherwood's *Gentleman's Choice* and *Feather Gatherers*. With Thaddeus Phillips he created *Red-Eye to Havre de Grace*, an action-opera about Edgar Allen Poe, which has been running for years in theaters across America. The story of Ean Sheehy's career is one of finding collaborators with whom he has a deep artistic connection, and with whom he can strike off into new theatrical territory.

Scott Shepherd is a longtime member of two of New York's leading theater companies, Elevator Repair Service (ERS) and The Wooster Group. In ERS's best-known piece, *Gatz*, a seven-hour staging of The Great Gatsby in which a man reads the entire book out loud at work, he was the man reading the entire book out loud. He played the title role in The Wooster Group's *Hamlet*, alongside a film of Richard Burton playing it in 1964. Scott has worked with directors Young Jean Lee, Annie Dorsen, Athol Fugard and Sam Gold, and directed several theater pieces himself. On screen, he has been a thorn in Tom Hanks' side, in Steven Spielberg's *Bridge of Spies*, and the Pope's best friend, in Paolo Sorrentino's *The Young Pope*. Other filmmakers he has worked with include Steven Soderbergh, Paul Greengrass, Rob Reiner, Jason Bateman, Meg Ryan and Hal Hartley. Also a programmer, Scott left a cybersecurity startup to join The Wooster Group in 2000. He has written language-transliteration software for The Wooster Group, Shakespeare-scrambling and and text-to-singing software for Annie Dorsen, and teleprompter and audio-cuing software for ERS.

Joseph Silovsky has been performing, constructing and collaborating in the theater world since 1990. He has performed shows at St. Ann's Warehouse, PS122, the Collapsable Hole and other venues in New York, as well as in Chicago and at the Kananahk Performance Art Festival in Rakveres, Estonia. His show *Send for the Million Men* premiered at HERE Arts Center in 2014, and was featured at Mass Live Arts Festival in Great Barrington, MA the following year. Other original works include: *The Jester of Tonga* at PS122, Binghamton First Night Festival, and elsewhere (2007- 2009); and *The Reddest Dirt in Oklahoma* at Abrons Art Center (2015) and Tonic's Little Theater (2006). Joseph has collaborated with Victor Morales as Tutto and the Ragman (2001-2005), as well as with Radiohole (2003-2013), The Builders Association (2000-2010), Lucky Pierre (1998-1999), HMS (1995-1997), and the Cook County Theater Department (1994). Joseph's robotic and/or mechanical creations for other companies' shows include: the mechanical moon for Radiohole's *Fluke* (2006) and *Anger Nation* (2008); the contest winning robot in NTUSA's *What's That on My Head!?!* (2004); the human-sized R/C robot for Richard Maxwell's *A-1 Rolling Steakhouse* (1999) and *Joe* (2002-2005); and both the sliding mechanical screens for The Builders Association's *Super Vision* (2005-6) and the butterfly screens for *Continuous City* (2007-2010). Silovsky received a BFA from Bard College in 1991 and went to graduate school for performance art at the School of the Art Institute of Chicago. Joseph has held residencies at Yaddo, DPI, LMCC and Mount Tremper Arts, and was a member of HERE's Artist in Residence Program (HARP) from 2012-2015. He has received grants from Art Matters, the Henson Foundation, the Puffin and the Axe-Haughton Foundations.

Pete Simpson has performed, written, composed and collaborated in New York's Off-Broadway and experimental theater scene since 1996. While completing his MFA in performance at the National Theater Conservatory in 1995, Pete was first introduced to east coast experimental theater at the Williamstown Theatre Festival by director Phil Soltanoff, who'd cast him as a principal in Chuck Mee's *The Trojan Women*. Upon graduation, Pete was immediately hired into the Boston production of the Blue Man Group. BMG's commercial success notwithstanding, it was a moment that confirmed his affinity for alternative/experimental theater. The following summer, again selected for the Williamstown Theater Festival, he deepened a still nascent attraction to experimental theater through his work with future Obie-winner Richard Maxwell. Pete went on to make his 'non-Blue' NYC acting debut as the lead in the experimental Bokanovsky Group's production of Vaclav Havel's *The Memorandum* in 1998, shortly thereafter also securing a coveted cast spot with the original NYC Blue Man Group production. His aesthetic mission officially transformed by these early exposures to experimental theater, Pete soon co-founded the experimental theater duo "Vad Voyghz" with fellow NTC grad Matt Schneck, a collaboration committed to dismantling expectations of theater audiences through subtle mutations of language, an absurdist filtering of basic semantic/logic rules and the meta-acknowledgement of both the observing audience and the theatrical devices/artificialities used in their work. Within his first year in NYC, Pete had the unusual fortune of landing principle roles with Richard Maxwell, Richard Foreman and The Wooster Group, work that subsequently opened the door to a string of principle performances, collaborations (including musical and choreographic) and creative dialogues with such artists as Young Jean Lee, Christina Masciotti, Big Dance Theater, Half Straddle, Susan Marshall, Elevator Repair Service and Julia Jarcho. Other performances or collaborations include those with Ken Rus Schmoll, Will Eno, Darko Tresnjak, Ethan Lipton and others. With the Blue Man Group, Pete celebrates over twenty years and over 4,000 performances, multiple direction/writing/training roles and appearances and recordings with artists such as David Bowie, Moby, Alicia Keys and Kodo percussion. Pete lives with his wife and two children in Brooklyn.

Lucy Taylor is an actor and theater maker who has been working in the downtown New York scene for a little over ten years. Born in England but raised in Australia. Lucy trained at the Drama School at the Victorian College of the Arts, where the emphasis was on training autonomous actors who could also be theater makers. It was here that she got her first taste of ensemble based generative theater, and on graduation went on to work with various directors and choreographers including Jenny Kemp, Neil Armfield, Michael Kantor and Jérôme Bel. In 2005 she moved to New York City and became a member of Elevator Repair Service, collaborating on the internationally renowned trilogy *Gatz*, *The Sound and the Fury* and *The Select (The Sun Also Rises)*. She was also in the cast of *Fondly, Collette Richland* which playwright Sibyl Kempson wrote for the company. Other recent collaborations have been with Tina Satter's company Half Straddle (*Ancient Lives*) and The Wooster Group (*The Town Hall Affair*). On screen she appeared in Louis CK's *Horace and Pete*.

Saori Tsukada was born in Washington state, and raised in Tokyo where she trained in classical ballet, gymnastics and cartoon making. She began working in theater while studying Visual Communication at Waseda University in Tokyo, where she moved from poster and costume design to choreography and then acting. Since moving to NYC in 1999, she has thrived in the downtown dance and theater scene, investing in her interests in movement-based methods such as clown, commedia, mask and puppetry. Between 2003 and 2011 she collaborated with her then-neighbor, composer/theater artist John Moran on works that were presented in NYC and throughout Europe, and for which Tsukada was nominated as Best Actress at Dublin Fringe Festival in '05 and '08. Tsukada has become known for her "astoundingly precise movements" (Irish Times) and "carefree charisma" (Village Voice), and has generated "virtuoso" (Time Out New York) roles for many stage works by the likes of Aya Ogawa, Yoshiko Chuma, Hoi Polloi, Shaun Irons and Lauren Petty, The Vintage DJ and Witness Relocation. Her ongoing collaborators include Catherine Galasso, Joe Diebes, Cathy Weis and Ripe Time. Her choreography works for the video artist Katja Loher have been exhibited and performed live at places like C24 Gallery (NYC), Figge Art Museum (Iowa) and the Contemporary Istanbul Art Fair. Her recent solo performance work, Club Diamond, co-created with Nikki Appino, featured original 16mm silent film and drawings and was premiered as part of the Public Theater's 2017 Under the Radar Festival.

Kate Valk is a performer and associate director with The Wooster Group. She joined the group in 1979 and since then has worked on all the group's theater and media pieces. Valk also founded The Wooster Group's Summer Institute for NYC public high school students.

Ben Williams is an actor and sound designer in New York City. He grew up in Culleoka, Tennessee, attended the University of Tennessee at Chattanooga, and got turned on to experimental theater while studying in the Czech Republic. In 2003, he moved to New York and began an internship with The Wooster Group. Shortly thereafter he began working with Elevator Repair Service—he would go on to perform in all of their shows for the next twelve years, touring across five continents and winning several awards for sound design (Obie, Lortel, Los Angeles Drama Critics Circle). Ben is also a founding member of minor theater with Julia Jarcho and has collaborated with many other downtown artists, including Christina Masciotti, Sibyl Kempson, Suzanne Bocanegra, Richard Maxwell and the NYC Players, Big Dance Theater, Kate Benson, Lee Sunday Evans and Lily Whitsitt. In a successful effort to stay one step ahead of a day job, Ben has embraced various technical aspects of theater, freelancing as a technical director, production manager, engineer and master carpenter. Occasionally, he works as a voice-over artist (theater, film, audiobooks). Building on his collaborations with playwrights, he serves as Editor of Performance Texts for *BODY*, an online literary journal, and has also freelanced as a ghostwriter. Recently, he has begun developing his own multimedia work.

Matthew Wilkas is a New York City-based actor and writer who most recently appeared in the title role of *Spider-Man* on Broadway. He is the star of the award-winning indie hit film *Gayby* and has worked extensively in Off-Broadway and regional theater, including work at the Williamstown Theatre Festival, the Huntington Theater, the Berkshire Theatre Festival, Rattlestick Theater and the Sundance Theatre Institute. On stage he has worked with directors Michael Greif, Anna D. Shapiro, Will Frears, Carolyn Cantor, Mark Brokaw, Nicholas Martin and Trip Cullman. His television credits include guest appearances on *Looking*, *Ugly Betty*, *Hope & Faith*, *All My Children*, *As the World Turns* and *Law & Order*. He also appeared in Chris Rock's film *Top Five*.

*Titles from 53rd State Press 2007-2017*

*The Book of the Dog // Karinne Keithley*

*Joyce Cho Plays // Joyce Cho*

*No Dice // Nature Theater of Oklahoma*

*Rambo Solo // Nature Theater of Oklahoma*

*When You Rise Up // Miguel Gutierrez*

*Montgomery Park, or Opulence // Karinne Keithley*

*Crime or Emergency // Sibyl Kempson*

*Off the Hozzle // Rob Erickson*

*A Map of Virtue and Black Cat Lost // Erin Courtney*

*Pig Iron: Three Plays // Pig Iron Theatre Company*

*The Mayor of Baltimore and Anthem // Kristen Kosmas*

*Ich, KürbisGeist and The Secret Death of Puppets // Sibyl Kempson*

*Soulographie: Our Genocides // Erik Ehn*

*Life and Times: Episode 1 // Nature Theater of Oklahoma*

*Life and Times: Episode 2 // Nature Theater of Oklahoma*

*Life and Times: Episodes 3 and 4 // Nature Theater of Oklahoma*

*The 53rd State Occasional No. 1 // Ed. Paul Lazar*

*Seagull (Thinking of you) // Tina Satter*

*There There // Kristen Kosmas*

*Another Telepathic Thing // Big Dance Theater*

*Another Tree Dance // Karinne Keithley Syers*

*Let Us Now Praise Susan Sontag // Sibyl Kempson*

*Pop Star Series // Neal Medlyn*

*The Javier Plays // Carlos Murillo*

*Minor Theater: Three Plays // Julia Jarcho*

*Ghost Rings (12-inch vinyl) // Half Straddle*

*Dance Pamphlet No. 1: Self Made Man Man Made Land // Ursula Eagly*

*Dance Pamphlet No. 2: Dance by Letter // Annie-B Parson*

*Dance Pamphlet No. 3: A Field Guide to iLANDing / / iLAND*

53rdstatepress.org